MEMOIRS, ANECDOTES, FACTS, AND OPINIO
LAETITIA MATILDA HAWKINS AND HENRY H

Publisher's Note

The book descriptions we ask booksellers to display prominently warn that this is an historic book with numerous typos or missing text; it is not indexed or illustrated.

The book was created using optical character recognition software. The software is 99 percent accurate if the book is in good condition. However, we do understand that even one percent can be an annoying number of typos! And sometimes all or part of a page may be missing from our copy of the book. Or the paper may be so discolored from age that it is difficult to read. We apologize and gratefully acknowledge Google's assistance.

After we re-typeset and design a book, the page numbers change so the old index and table of contents no longer work. Therefore, we often remove them; otherwise, please ignore them.

Our books sell so few copies that you would have to pay hundreds of dollars to cover the cost of our proof reading and fixing the typos, missing text and index. Instead we let most customers download a free copy of the original typo-free scanned book. Simply enter the barcode number from the back cover of the paperback in the Free Book form at www.RareBooksClub.com. You may also qualify for a free trial membership in our book club to download up to four books for free. Simply enter the barcode number from the back cover onto the membership form on our home page. The book club entitles you to select from more than a million books at no additional charge. Simply enter the title or subject onto the search form to find the books.

If you have any questions, could you please be so kind as to consult our Frequently Asked Questions page at www. RareBooksClub.com/faqs.cfm? You are also welcome to contact us there.
General Books LLC™, Memphis, USA,

2012. ISBN: 9781150152252.

-- -- -- -- -- -- -- --

ENGLISH OXFORD LIBRARY ENGLISH LIBRARY *Temporary Address:*
Examination Schools,
High Street, Oxford.
This book should be returned on or before the latest date below: MEMOIRS.
VOL. I.
London.
  Printed by A. & R. Spottiswoode.
  New-Street-Square.
MEMOIRS,
ANECDOTES, FACTS,
AND
OPINIONS,
COLLECTED AND PRESERVED
BY
LTITIA-MATILDA HAWKINS.
IX TWO VOLUMES.
VOL. I.
I am a great advocate for bringing in by head, neck, and shoulders. *Ex ore. G.* Steevens.
LONDON:
PRINTED FOR
LONGMAN, HURST, REES, ORME, BROWN, AND GREEN;
AND C. & J. RIVINGTON.
1824.,
ADVERTISEMENT.

  The two Volumes now published, under the title of "Memoirs, Anecdotes, Facts, and Opinions," may be considered as a continuation of the Volume already published by me, entitled "Anecdotes, Biographical Sketches, and Memoirs:" the alteration of title has been at the suggestion of the publishers.

  L. M. H.

  A d TO DR. FERGUSSON, OF WINDSOR.
MY DEAR SIR,

  I Know not to whom any effort of industry can with more propriety be offered, than to him who, under Heaven, gave the power of exertion.

  This being an obligation to you, which I am happy to acknowledge, allow me to prefix your name to this Vol-

Twickenham, 24th June, 1824.
TABLE OF CONTENTS.
VOLUME I.
I fear I have somewhere promised an *Index* to these volumes.

  On consideration, the form now adopted is preferred.

MEMOIRS.

I Should break a tacit compact with the public— I dare not say, I should disappoint *expectation*— were I to consider myself as having concluded the little work of recollection, of which they have so kindly accepted one volume; but the difficulty I feel in working by a pattern, will I hope excuse me, if, in resuming my endeavour to preserve small things from oblivion, I depart in some degree from my original *intention;* for plan I cannot presume to consider as entering into any of the casualties that *my* pen produces.

My first duty is to correct my errors; therefore I have to acknowledge the receipt of a very polite letter from Miss Knight, dated from Paris, in which she professes her absolute ignorance of any such roughness of speech from Dr. Johnson on her taking leave of him to quit England, as I have reported of him; and, on the contrary, speaks, with grateful remembrance, of the unvarying gentleness and kindness of his language to her at all times.

A friend, also, thinks me inaccurate with regard to Boswell's bitterness towards my father. I can reply to this only by referring, I confess with a smile, to a subsequent edition of Mr. B.'s Life of Johnson, in which he professes himself to have some feelings of compassion towards Sir J. H. since his decease. Why these feelings *at any time,* if those previously indulged were just?

Another mistake I have made, as one of Dr. Cooke's family informs me, in saying that Dr. C. was liberal of copies from the library of the academy of ancient music, when held at the Crown and Anchor Tavern. I am assured that he had no such power. I can only plead then that Sir J. H. himself was mistaken, for I have heard him mention it as one of the circumstances which led to the unforeseen undermining of the establishment.

As I have myself felt as a great grievance that improvement of a work in reprinting it, which diminishes the value of the original, I prefer placing corrections and inserting additions to the former volume, in *this,* rather than taxing the reader by a new purchase.

After a long cessation, it is very difficult to resume a desultory narrative without repeating or omitting; I' will therefore endeavour to bring together what I know of those of my father's earliest connections, of whom I retain particulars which I have not yet recorded.

I remember from the time of my earliest recollection, a very gentlemanly man whom I have yet only named, and this was Alexander Scott: he was an Irishman, and, as I have hinted before, had travelled with Lord Charlemont — consequently his name will be found in His Lordship's Memoirs. His features were rather strongly marked, and gave him no pretensions to be called handsome; but his figure and person were more than commonly fine, and in the manly exercises he was a pattern. He was a horseman of the old riding-school, and by daily practice retained, to the age of more than eighty, the power to do feats of extraordinary agility. Riding with the son of an old neighbour, and being reminded by him that he had been famous for being able to pick up a half-crown piece from the ground, when on some considerable speed, Mr. Scott replied, "I used indeed to do it, and I believe I could now:" he then spurred his horse, which was one that required a powerful master, threw down the half-crown, and performed the feat with perfect ease.

He was the first traveller of whom I heard, as having visited the Pyramids;

and when he talked to me of them, he probably had to tell me what they were: but his conversation was always attractive, even to a child, and the sound of his voice is still in my ear. As I grew up, I enjoyed extremely those now despised *soirees* in which a few persons met, without any pretensions to conversation, but to partake of each other's society. Alas! such intercourse is now gone—the noise of large assemblies drums down everything but those rapid enquiries and observations which not only do not require but do not admit of reply.—" I never visit where I do not eat," is a very coarse justification of the exclusive love of dinners. Eating does not further the relating of, or the listening to, that which one person may be able to tell, and another may wish to hear. Music, dancing, and cards, are all good at times and seasons; but surely their prosperity does not require the *entire* sacrifice of that intercourse in which interest was excited and attention was fixed, if a veteran in the world would unlock the stores of his active days, and when the young were kindly encouraged to hear, without being frightened at the sound of their own voice.

It is with a sense of good fortune that I recollect a better state of things, when Alexander Scott would give to his conversation a pliancy that made every one by turns his hearer. Instead of yawning and enquiring for the carriage, under the dull inflictions of what may more properly be termed *parades* than *parties,* the hour for separating always came too soon; what had been heard made an impression, and such impressions furnished such volumes as this.

I remember particularly one evening meeting at Mr. Scott's a gentleman of his own christian and surname, with whom some mistake, occasioned by this singular resemblance, had brought him acquainted. He had been in the service of government, in a capacity not perhaps the most honourable, but requiring talents of a peculiar kind; and one incident he related which had in itself more importance than I could then understand: he was employed by our ministry

to ascertain the intentions of the court of France, with regard to the marriage of the then Dauphin, afterwards the unhappy Louis XVI. Such secrecy was observed on this important point, that nothing positive could be hoped for, through any medium. The *definitive* intention could be obtained from no one but the minister himself, the Due de Choiseul, not a personage very likely to be guilty of a political blunder, or to leave his despatches in a hackney coach.

But the thing must be done, and it *was* done; for this *double* to my father's friend, this Alexander Scott the second, obtained admission into the Due de Choiseul's private apartment of business, and mounting behind a large folding screen, he made himself acquainted with the papers on his table, as far as their external superscriptions could inform him. After long watching, he at length saw him open what he could see was the outline of the projected union of the Dauphin with the Archduchess of Austria, afterwards the miserable Marie-Antoinette. He had then seen enough, and had only to observe where the document was deposited. As soon as the Duke quitted the room, he left his place of concealment, and not, as might be expected, taking minutes of the treaty, but possessing himself of the treaty itself, he returned to his employers, who were enabled to act on the information. This, I doubt not, is little in comparison with what is sometimes achieved by those employed on such service; but it is curious as authentic and circumstantial. A service of much more personal danger, I have heard my father say, old Mr. Carrington *the kings messenger,* as couriers were then called, had performed, when, *to* convey cash into a besieged town, he had to creep through an aperture in a wall within range of point-blank shot, the enemy firing at him.

The commissions to foreign countries, with which *heralds* are sometimes charged, are of a far different nature, and such as ladies would like to share in. I myself have lost some of these opportunities by a most inconvenient and

almost blameable fear of the sea; but there is one little narrative which I could give, and which would prove what I have said, and perhaps gratify the reader, could I record circumstances without An occurrence nearly coeval with the intimacy I have recorded, served to show, in rather a ludi taking improper liberties or giving offence. I am unwilling to suppress my narrative: what shall I do? This I will do: I will not print a name which I have not a right to use; the owner then may challenge it if he pleases, and I will change a name where the owner may take offence. If *he* betrays *himself,* it is not *my* fault. As to correctness of relation, I copy from what I heard, and wrote down with the intervention of only an hour or two.'

In August, 1813, a herald was sent to invest the Russian Emperor Alexander with the order of the Garter. It was mortifying in the extreme, to Garter King at Arms, that he was thought too far advanced in years for the mission. An officer of the Order had written to him an unqualified opinion, that " he was *too old* to be sent;" but this humiliating rejection was graciously softened by a letter from a Higher Power, *advising* him not to undertake, at his time of life, a business which might involve him in trouble and fatigue. This soothed the old man, who, may I be allowed to say, was perhaps less unequal to the task than he was deemed, for he lived in wondrous vigour for several years, and died in 1822 at the age of upwards of ninety.

Our friend, the herald, was sent in his stead; and considering the then political state of Europe, some curiosity may be excited to know exactly his proceedings in reaching the Emperor's head-quarters, then at Toplitz in Bohemia.

He sailed from Yarmouth, and was obliged to go through Sweden into Germany, by way of Stralsund, and. thence sent a courier forward to our minister, Lord C, advising him that he was on the road. The answer which he received, signified the Emperor's wish that he would remain at Prague, crous than a luminous point of view, the disposition to oppose, when the public good is till the place at which he should finally rest, should be notified to him. To Prague therefore he went, and there would have remained, had he not been thwarted by a personage, whom we will call Count, who, without any appointment, had attached himself to the mission. This personage havinc: heard that a *gala* in honour of Alexander was to take place at Toplitz, was in his own mind persuaded, that it would be felt as a proper compliment that the mission should *proceed,* in order that the investiture might make part of this splendid *fete.* In a council on the question, our herald found himself in a minority; he therefore yielded so far as to proceed within one stage of Toplitz.

In consideration of his own rank, the Count had striven through the whole journey to keep the lead, that he might evade giving precedence; and this solicitude occasionally produced something amusing. In his wish to *go* first, because he had no right to *be* anywhere, he always sacrificed the credit he sought, of belonging to the mission. His own coachman, not being in the exercise of his office, sate in a 'seat behind; he was thrown off, and his collar-bone broken. Our herald, who was coming up, saw the accident, and stopping the carriages, got out, and lent his assistance to remove the man to the side of the road. The Count's surgeon travelled with him, and he bled the man, our herald remaining to assist, while the sufferer's illustrious employer walked about to avoid the 6ight of blood. The man must now be put *into* one of the carriages, and in the exigency, was placed in that of his master. This, perhaps, merely because done unceremoniously, the Count disapproved: he would not again enter the carriage: the poor fellow, from whom nothing of in question; but, to *he just,* I believe I ought to treat this spirit as going out of fashion.

this scrupulosity was concealed, begged to be put out again, but this could not be. The Count, therefore, took the carriage of the *avant courier,* and made him to whom it belonged ride with the invalid; consequently, in all the towns through which they passed, the respect due to the Count himself was paid to his equipage, and its subordinate occupiers. Arrived at the inn where they were to pass the night, he sate in abstraction, with his face to the wall; and though he had usually regulated the meals of the mission, he now gave notice to those who composed it, that they might cater for themselves, for he was too much annoyed to do it.

From the place beyond which no resolution of council could induce our herald to go, the Count, whom nothing restrained, set forward in his travelling carriage at the most expeditious rate, that if he did not *lead* into Toplitz, he might *get there first.* But there he soon learned his error, and that he should have given credit to the suggestion which had been urged, that a man so free from ostentation as Alexander, and of such kind consideration for others, would avoid all unnecessary publicity in receiving an honour which the other allied sovereigns could not share with him.

On its being notified, however, that Count, who was supposed of the mission, was arrived, the Emperor's horses and servants were immediately sent for the herald, who, in his first interview with the British minister, heard that in leaving Prague they had passed the *chateau* preparing for the ceremony, and that at Toplitz it was almost impossible that they could be accommodated even with lodgings. The Emperor had given up the two best houses to the Emperor of Austria and the King of Prussia, and contented himself with a very

The improvements in London within the last seven years, imply great sacrifices of individual poor residence. The gentlemen, therefore, slept, some on chairs and some on the floor.

The investiture took place after the *gala,* consequently at a late hour, in a small room, and with not more *of cortege* than was requisite.

The presents were sent to the lodings of the gentlemen of the mission. In these the volunteer Count could have no share. Our herald had a gold box, of an oblong form, set superbly with table diamonds of a very large size, with two brilliants filling up the corners between every two diamonds. This setting enclosed a miniature of the Emperor exquisitely painted. One of our first goldsmiths, who was sent by authority to see the present at a pattern for our court on similar occasions, declared that the box might be copied, but that no such miniature could be painted in this country. The sky is of the tenderest purple, receding round the portrait into the most celestial blue; and it is supposed that the ivory is more than usually thin, and much of the color laid on the back. I should have said that the large diamonds are fortyeight in number; that the inside of the box is burnished, and the outside chased with fruit and flowers of the most delicate workmanship.

I hope my reader is as much disposed as I am, to hear everything that an authentic informer can tell, or I shall have no pardon for supposing *she*—for I cannot expect the attention of any *he* — may like to know, that on the day after the investiture, our herald dined with the Emperor, sitting opposite to him, with *General Bennigsen* on his right hand!

convenience, and the murmurs heard have not been loud or deep. But in the instance to which

The Emperor's conversation may also, I trust, prove interesting, though I cannot convey the tone and action with which it was given to me, and which indicated the cordial sensibility of a man whose natural goodness deserves to be seen through a better medium than that of politics.

In the course, then, I will say, of this dinner, the Emperor related in English the circumstances of General Moreau's death. "We were riding together," said he, " and coming to an awkward bit of road, he told me he would show me a better way. I pulled up my horse, (using the action of reining in the horse,) to give him the lead,—and—the shot took *him."*

Speaking of the situation of the allied forces as opposed to Bonaparte, he said, " We have him now in such a situation, that unless we ourselves are guilty of some great blunder, which I hope we shall not be, we *must* conquer."

In this ceremonial investiture, an English gentleman hold-' ing a situation under government, had procured himself an appointment. His mother had been one of the ladies who, at the request of the Czarina, had been sent out from England to systematise, if I may so say, the royal nurseries of St. Petersburgh: he himself had been a play-fellow of Alexander's, and enjoyed a pension, and whether he had or had not any hopes or views, the opportunity presented what was too important to be lost. He was walking on a causeway by the roadside, when by chance he met the three sovereigns on horseback, with their *suite.* The Emperor instantly knew him: he spurred his horse, rode up to him, and said, "Why, it *mint* be you—you must be . Who would have thought of our meeting thus? i, Emperor of I allude, they were not merely murmurs. The subject was nothing more than the new paving a

Russia, and *you* coming to me on so agreeable an occasion! How are you? — What are you? — Married? — Children?"

Proceeding in his enquiries, Mr. having said that he was the father of seven children, felt encouraged to add, "The pension with which Your Majesty honoured me, must drop with me." "Jamais, jamais," replied Alexander, interrupting him, "je gage mon honneur." Then turning back to the two English noblemen in his train, he said, " When you return home, I request you to say to your Prince Regent, that any favour shown to this gentleman, I shall be glad to acknowledge as done *to* myself."

May I be indulged in telling one of those pretty stories of this good-natured sovereign, which make him appear the son of a much softer climate than that in which he was bom? An English family went to reside in Russia, and taking their servants with them, lived as in England. At Christmas, they made mince-pies; and a Russian gentleman tasting them, thought the introduction of this new dish into the Emperor's kitchen would be agreeable. Alexander having found the mince-pies very palatable, enquired how the recipe had been pro-

cured; and being informed that Mrs., the wife of an

English gentleman, had sent the minced meat ready for use, he called on her in the most familiar way, and expressed himself very desirous to return her kindness. Finding her in HI health, and learning that she had accompanied her husband in hope of benefit from the climate, he told her that he had a very quiet little horse, just suited to an invalid, which should always be at her service; and every morning during her residence, this horse was at her door. On her return to England, he sent her a gold watch set with diamonds street, which grievously needed it; and my father, as an inhabitant of one of the best houses in it, as a magistrate for the county, and a commissioner for the business, exerted himself to have it done in the best way. To do this, he set the example of accommodating himself to the necessity; but there were others who stickled for the remaining of stone posts, and the disregard of level that they might still enter their houses by a rising step or two. One gentleman, I remember, whose house had stood two inches above the foot-pavement, was extremely incensed, on finding that nothing but a broad flat stone would be left him: he declared, that the entrance to his house would be "like going into a cellar to drink broth;" and though others might express their feelings in superior language, the feelings were nearly the Of this tenacity a strong proof was given in Milan, when Bonaparte, who, to do him justice, had a good taste for bettering the condition of some things, ordered the inhabitants, against his next visit, to make their doors open inwards instead of outwards, as they did then to the general obstruction of passengers. They would have resisted had they dared; but as they dared *not,* they obtained what they now deem a blessed improvement same; and this unfortunate business of giving to a street then esteemed one of the best in London the advantage of a good pavement, occasioned such heart-burning and enmity, that it broke up long-standing friendships, and made strangers of those who,

before this time, had been in the habit of almost daily intercourse.

The same thing occurred at Twickenham, when my father was earnest to coincide with the surveyors of the highway in removing nuisances. It will now hardly be credited that there stood, in my earliest memory, in the road leading from the church to the ferry, narrow enough at all times, a double, flight of stone steps, projecting about four feet into the road: they were only a back-entrance to a What must Mr. M'Adam have had to endure in his improvements, had this spirit prevailed till now? But, fortunately for him, there is more good sense in the world. He is eulogised by all the proprietors of stage-coaches and post-horses; and on the road to Oxford, I was told, when changing horses at Tetsworth a few months ago, that "they soon should do away all the hills. " And here I may record, lest it may not reach posterity, the brilliant sentiment of a gentleman at a public dinner, who, when a toast was given, " The Colossus of Literature, Sir Walter Scott," returned it with,« The Colossus of Roads, Mr. M'Adam." garden; and the owners of the house keeping a carriage, an elderly couple, and uniformly coming out at their front-gates, could seldom recollect that they *had* these steps, but the removing them for the public safety was an offence not to be endured. Fashion, however, in a few years, did the office of humanity: entrances from the riverside of our great villas were voted plebeian, and not one is to be seen where another entrance can be used.

It is this proof of a fallen nature which paralyses the endeavours of the good and the wise to correct abuses. "I shall make so many enemies," is the common excuse for not acting as a magistrate, and, consequently, the lords of misrule are the lords of the creation. But I have lived to hear my father wished alive; and have more than once been stopped to be shown the evil that has *crept* in, or rather *broke* in, for want of his firm spirit.

For this spirit he had occasion, in the season of what are called Wilkes's riots, and in the insurrections of the Sailors and Weavers in London. In one of the latter calls on the county-magistracy, he was under the necessity of holding a conference with the malcontents in Moorfields, at a time when the extensive space so called, was the repository for the stones of the old pavement of London. Their weapons were thus at hand; and my father presented himself, perfectly aware of this advantage against him. He had a good person, at that time rather commanding, and a voice well toned to gain attention; and he had uttered but a few words, when the ringleader of the sailors proposed hearing what the gentleman had to say, and the rest, making a fence of their bludgeons, became rather his guard than his assailants.

When I speak of these situations, I do not mean to state that he stood a solitary individual; he had the peace-officers around him, and perhaps some of his " brethren," as they were then worthy to be styled. The commission of the peace for the most important county in England, did not then stand as low in talents or estimation as it did afterwards, when it was a disgrace to those who had the power of appointing, and the right of recommending,—when it included men of just ability enough to be proud of opposing, and when its members, as old Colonel Brettell, the stoutesthearted and the strongest-headed amongst them, used to say, had picked up a little knowledge, by attending on special juries, and thought themselves lawyers. I must do George Steevens the justice to say, that he had so due a sense of the responsibility of the situation, as to keep his name out of the commission. I heard him say, " Men cannot be made intuitively lawyers."

H. H. adds, "Some of these magistrates might be seen at one time presiding at Hicks's Hall, and in the next term attending the court of King's Bench to receive sentence for corruption in the situation of trading justices, —a situation not known, since the salutary establishment of police offices.— A happy change I confess, brother, for the metropolis; but, in saying this, you might have adverted to the cruel unconcern

with which the legislature leave such a village as Twickenham in an utterly lawless state. Two or three miles off, we *may* chance to find redress for *great* grievances; but for general and daily police it is vain to seek. So near the metropolis, we need looking after. Distinguished by rank, wealth, and the highest tone of society, we need to be guarded while we are off our guard; and offering, as we do, little short of premiums to beggars, we take exercise in peril almost of our lives. Surely every village should have its magistrate: — and surely there ought to be some authority to prevent or punish the uniform breach of a commandment in employing gardeners and carpenters in the subordinate classes, to trim up flowerbeds, and do small repairs, before church time on Sundays."

I state this only to introduce some curious facts. It used to be said of one of them, whose name was David, and who had been a bricklayer at the east end of the town, where, by prescription, these *justices* were of the lowest order, that he never wrote more of his baptismal name than the two first letters, having a doubt in his mind as to one of the subsequent ones. I myself heard this personage say, that he had "breakfasted on such a day with government, and that his daughter was going to send to government's daughter a present of a pair of turtle-doves." Lest any question should arise as to the identity of government, I must inform the reader, that in this acceptation of the term it means the secretary to the prime minister.

There was, however, a species of amiability about this worshipper of the ruling powers. He was soft in his manners; and if my father was at all less informed than was requisite to understanding him, he would patiently explain. For instance: — talking one day of "the generals," he saw that he was not perfectly clear; he therefore spoke more diffusely, and said, "There are two generals, the soliciting general and the returning general." Sir J. H. thanked him for the trouble he had taken; they were now on equal terms, and could get on.

Another of these wights, while Sir J.

H. was sitting as chairman at the sessions-house, Hicks's Hall , came to him, and with great formality presented him with a small volume, very thick and very expensively bound, like a prayer book.— My father received it with acknowledgments; but what was his surprise, when he found it only the Court Calendar of the time, with an almanac prefixed to it! How the donor became possessed of such a bauble I cannot tell, unless his holding the situation of lamplighter to his Majesty entitled him to it. An abuse in the distribution of these perquisites, which has, I dare say, been corrected; for I have heard of yearly publications of this kind, fitted up for those holding superior situations, to the expense of thirty pounds.

In a very few years a question will be asked, if it be not asked already, Where was Hicks's Hall? For those passing the spot, there is indeed information on a stone placed to commemorate its existence. It was a mean old building, situated in St. John's Street, Clerkenwell, and named from Sir Baptist Hicks, who built it on crown land, about the year 1610, for the purpose to which it was applied.

In speaking irreverently of these dispensers of public justice, I must repeat, that those whom my father found in the commission, were of a better order and description. But the American war had brought on exigencies which, sad to say! compelled the government to employ *useful* persons. Sir J.'s predecessor had been a Master in Chancery; and many gentlemen of landed property acted as magistrates when he took the office. It was, therefore, extremely vexatious to my father to see himself afterwards surrounded with such as I have described; and those whom I have mentioned were not, as the subsequent reform proved, the very worst. Sir J. did all in his power to keep the commission, as he termed it, "*pure*" but his efforts were vain; and I can now regret that he did not, on the first failure of a justifiable remonstrance, resign his situation. One man, who was literally proprietor of a register office for servants, assailed him incessantly with solicitations and presents, which were discouraged and refused as soon as their motive was discovered; but by a subterfuge he prevailed.

The reader's attention to what, perhaps, is little interesting, may be relieved by the recital of a curious instance of the case of bribes, as a mean of success. Sir J. and Lady H. were on the road to London from Twickenham, when their lives were seriously endangered, by the brutality of a stage-coachman, who wantonly drove his heavy-laden vehicle against their chariot, and with so much violence, as to bend the wheel-iron, and wrench the handle from the door. On their coachman's remonstrating, he was silenced by the grossest abuse, and blinded by two cuts across the face with the whipcord. The bystanders most willingly encouraged a disposition to punish such an unprovoked outrage: they informed my father of the man's name, and to what place the coach belonged; and some could add that the driver was a nuisance on the road. Sir J. was, perhaps, one of the last persons that such an offender should have attacked: he could have no doubt or scruple; and having declared that, at any trouble or expense, he would make an example of such a public culprit, he went the shortest way to do it. But the man got intelligence of his danger, and first kept out of sight, hiring a man to drive for him, and then changed his situation, and was no more seen on that road. But my father knew mankind well enough to surmise that the sense of danger once abated, he would revisit his old haunts. He therefore kept Lord Mansfield's tipstaves on the watch at the White-horse Cellar, and one of them had the satisfaction of seeing him enter the kitchen, where he was soon recognised by those of his own stamp. Each told what had occurred since they last met; and he had to account for his temporary invisibility, which he did by an exulting description of his heroic deed, particularly dwelling on the vengeance he had taken on the coachman. He had now furnished evidence in abundance—he was beckoned out, and handcuffed j and at the next quarter sessions tried,

Sir J. H. appearing only as prosecutor: his sentence was six months' imprisonment in Newgate, and a small fine to the coachman. And as soon as the sentence was carried into effect, my father was attacked on all sides with letters and petitions; and probably by some of those who had volunteered their evidence. It was strongly urged that the time of his imprisonment would preclude him from the gains of Christmas; but nothing speeding, he, as a *dernier ressort,* sent my father a brace of partridges!

The false compassion of the present day may blame this as vindictive, but Sir J. H. had the thanks of many for persevering in an act of justice.

To return to the Middlesex magistracy. One pretender to the dignity made to Sir J. a very energetic representation of his claims; *he* had had the honour to obtain a prize in His Majesty's lottery: he signed himself *esquire.* I laughed at this representative of Shakspeare's Master Slender; but I confess, were his example followed, it would be very convenient. It is impossible in *our* mode of subscribing ourselves, to convey an idea of the manner in which our correspondent is to address us in return, unless we make an untoward statement of our *style.* The French manage much better: rank i$ expressed if necessary, and trouble is saved. But even this has its matter of offence. I knew an elderly widow lady, who dealing sometimes with quakers, received their bills made out to her as "The widow , debtor to," &c. I was with her when one of these unceremonious billets arrived: she indignantly sent it back, saying, "I will not be described by my misfortune."

Various stories are told of the mistakes against which I would guard,—of letters received from "George Winton,"

One great but fruitless effort my father made to have expunged from the commission a name, which, as a name, was certainly, in its connections of blood and alliance, an honour to the magistracy—but the gentleman had won from a young man in the line of succession to a ducal title, a very large sum of money. There could be no doubt on the question, or the mode of proce-

dure in it; but it was out of his power to bring that have taxed the recollection of *great men;* of an official letter directed to " S. Dunelm, Esq." puzzling the clerks of the post office; and of wine sent, most carefully packed, directed, and shipped for " Messrs. Cork and Ossory." May I be permitted to close this note with an amusing anecdote of the noble personage above mentioned as *the loser?* When arrived at the *acme* of his honours, he retained the social habits of his juvenile years; and one day suddenly crossing on the gentleman whom I have already characterised as "Our Herald," he stopt his chariot, to propose to him the enjoyment of a tavern-dinner. Naming, as the place of meeting, the Crown and Anchor, which in consequence of a sudden death was not then under its usual regular management, a question was started, whether the wine, just in that time of confusion, could be relied on: "I know not," replied his Grace, "what it may be at this moment,—I never found it do *me* any harm but *once."*

This *once* will be recognised by persons informed as that time and day of licentiousness, when "The Majesty of the People" was his Grace's toast. It certainly did him no good.

c those who had the authority to act as it was their duty to do. I must, however, except the Lord Lieutenant of the county; and I think, if I remember right, that Lord Mansfield, whom he saw often on the business, gave him his assistance. It is to the credit of the nation if I am not believed when I say, that the issue of this endeavour was a peevish complaint of being "teazed," from the exalted personage who should have done the requisite act, and finally a civil note, saying that he was sorry "he could not comply with Sir J. H.'s wish in *this* point, but should be very happy to oblige him in any other." As if Sir J. H. was seeking any thing but the public good, or could be bribed into a corrupt connivance.

I was interested in all these occurrences, not as in themselves interesting to *me,* but as they added to my almost incessant task of copying, or writing from dictation previous to copying. One remains deeply impressed on my memory, as peculiarly laborious to me and vexatious to my employer.

Sir J. H. had tried a man for an assault on a sheriff's officer. I do not know whether the offence would not *now* be deemed *capital,* as it consisted in stabbing the man near the stomach. The culprit was, either by profession or trade, of the lower order of medical men: he was cutting sassafras with a knife, and made this use of it to defend his own person.

My father saw the offence in two points of view, as an atrocious resistance to authority, and as connected with a most dangerous principle of conduct. The man was found guilty, and sentenced to two years' imprisonment in Newgate. He petitioned the Crown, and my father had the usual letter from the Secretary of State, commanding him to report upon the case: he did so, but was very much surprised to find that, contrary to all usage, it was wished that he would reconsider his opinion; and above all, when he had done so, and only strengthened his report by argument, to hear that the remission of the sentence was to be looked for.

While the matter was agitating over his head, solicitation to himself was not spared. The man set every engine to work, and somehow interested in his behalf a person of the name of Hutton, then at the head of the society of Moravians, occupying the very large house near the Middlesex foot of Battersea bridge, then called Lindsey House, now divided into many small dwellings. I had the perusal of a most curious epistle, in pathetic bombast, which this advocate addressed to the lady of Sir Charles Whitworth, to obtain his mediation with my father. It began thus: "Will Lady Whitworth, in some easy moment," &c. &c. Her ladyship forwarded the supplication; and I remember Sir Charles's bringing it to my father: but I fancy he saw the propriety of leaving the law to take its course.

An intimation that, if thus unreasonably counteracted, he should immediately quit the situation he held, was the last resource, and this succeeded: but

while the offender was wearing out his sentence, carriages that told too much, were, by eight in the morning, seen at the door of Newgate; and, on *i* enquiry, my father learnt that the Moravian trafficked in that favorite commodity " small diamonds." I hope my reader has a great curiosity to hear, what I can tell about the beforementioned Lindsey House, and its neighbourhood — at least, I must *suppose* it, as I wish to preserve the intelligence which I took pains to gain from "Old Howard the Quaker," then the living record of the spot. In his memory it was inhabited by a Duchess of Rutland, whose grandchildren are now living; but it had been the residence of Hortensia Mancini, the niece of Cardinal Mazarin, known in England as Duchess of Mazarin, and who was sent hither with her profligate but witty attendant, St. Evremond, on one of the *righteous* commissions of the French government of that period.

I will borrow from my father's History of Music, a memoir of this celebrated lady, whose portrait graces the beauty-room of Strawberry Hill, and an obscure apartment of Hampton-Court Palace.

"Hortensia Mancini was one of the four daughters of Lorenzo Mancini, by Jeronima Mazarin, sister of Cardinal Mazarin. She had been in France from the time that she was six years of age; and improving in wit and beauty, attracted the regard of the whole court. King Charles II. saw her at Paris, and more than once demanded her in marriage; but the Cardinal, seeing no prospect of his restoration, refused his consent, though he lived to repent it; and in 1661 married her to the Duke de la Meilleraie, with whom she lived about four years, without reproach; but upon a disagreement with him, she left him possessed of the fortune which the Cardinal had bequeathed to her, amounting to twenty millions of livres; and in 1675, having been invited hither with a view to supplant the Duchess of Portsmouth in the King's affections, she came into England; where she was scarcely arrived, before the King settled on her an annual pension of four thousand pounds: and there was little doubt

but she would have answered the end of her being sent for; but in the following year the Prince of Monaco arriving here, she was so negligent of her business as to engage in an amour with him; which coming to the King's ear, he withdrew her pension, and was hardly prevailed on to restore it. She had other intrigues upon her hands at different times; which are not to be wondered at. In the Memoirs of her life, written by the Abbe de St. Real, but under her own immediate direction, it is related that the Cardinal, her uncle, was much displeased with her and her sister Madame de Bouillon, for their want of de votion; and that once complaining to them that they did not hear mass every day, he told them that they had neither piety nor honour; adding this exhortation, which deserves to be remembered, 'At least, if you will not hear mass for God's sake, do it for the world's.'

"But the want of religious principle in this lady, seems, in the opinion of her panegyrists, especially Monsieur St. Erremond, to have been amply atoned for, by her wit and beauty. This person, who had a considerable hand in the laudable business of bringing her hither, almost always resided in her house, which, if we may believe the accounts that are given of her manner of living, was a kind of academy, and daily frequented by the principal nobility, and persons distinguished for wit and genius, where, in the style of free conversation, were discussed subjects of the deepest speculation, such as philosophy and religion, history, poetry, criticism on dramatic and other compositions, and the niceties of the French language. And that nothing might be wanting to increase the attractions of this bower of bliss, the game of basset was introduced, and an obscure man, named Morin, permitted to keep a bank in it; and concerts were given there, in which St. Evremond himself set the music: indeed, if we enquire into his share of the musical composition, his attempts in this way must appear ridiculous; for we are told, though he composed tunes to his own verses, and particularly to sundry idylls, and other pieces of his writing, yet that as to overtures, chorusses, and symphonies, he left them to some able musician, who, we elsewhere learn, was Paisible, a composer for the flute.

"St. Evremond, though an old man, was blind to the follies, and even vices of this woman, whom we may style the modern Cleopatra, and has disgraced himself by the fulsome praises of her,. with which his works abound. He wrote the words to most of the vocal compositions performed at her house, and generally presided at the performance. The Duchess died in 1699, aged fifty-two.

"The musical representations at the Duchess of Mazarin's were chiefly dramatic, and are celebrated for their magnificence. The singers in them were women from the theatres; and the instrumental performers the most eminent masters of the time. It is supposed that the design of introducing the Italian Opera into England, was first concerted in this assembly. The death of the Duchess retarded but for a few years the carrying it into execution; for in 1707, the opera of Arsinoe, consisting of English words adapted *to* Italian airs, by Mr. Thomas Clayton, was performed at Drury Lane theatre; and a succession of entertainments of this kind terminated in the establishment of an opera properly so called, in which the drama was written in the Italian language, and the music in the Italian style of composition."

We are all disposed to exhort those who fell a tree, to plant another in its stead, to console us for the loss of an old friend; but there is no consolation for the destruction of buildings which have borne great names, or been the nest of remarkable deeds; on the contrary, an indignant feeling of jealousy is excited by the upstart successor of a venerable mansion, and we take time to be reconciled even to improvement. All that can be done An Italian Opera is mentioned in Mr. Evelyn's Diary, 1674, perhaps an experiment. is to preserve graphic representations, and verbal descriptions — all, alas! inadequate to keeping in the mind's eye the recollection of that which while it existed we fancied we never could for-

get. In the present improvements of those middle parts of London, formerly distinguished as the *west end,* how long will St. Alban's Street, the venerable tavern, St. James's Market, and many other places of equal notoriety be present to our ideas? What a work of circumlocution would it be to describe the situation of Bedford House in Bloomsbury Square! and who will believe that to meet behind Montagu House , was a periphrasis for a challenge in the *Jklds* behind the British Museum; or give any credit to the legend of "the wonderful steps," as awfully recording in the obstinate barrenness of the earth, the vindictive quarrel of two brothers who fought on the provocation of a few idle words! A deep feeling on this subject makes me refer to collections made at a very early period of my life, not merely from books, but *viva voce* from persons, whom long life and retentive memories The external part of the building now existing is as old as 1677. made chronicles; and I always found them pleased to be listened to, in the indulgence of feelings similar to those which excited my inquisitiveness. Chelsea was a place very prolific in this species of lore, but rendered peculiarly open to dilapidation, by the building the bridge to Battersea — a convenience in all situations purchased by a great sacrifice of landmarks.

The greatest spoil was of Beaufort House, which in the print engraved by Kip, appears connected with a great extent of profitable garden and pleasureground. The print, which gives a bird's-eye view, places in the northern distance, Holland House, Campden House, and Kensington Palace, all well described by Lysons. The next range of situations below, includes houses in Little Chelsea, and amongst them, we may presume, that of Mr. Locke, whose summer-house is probably yet standing; an extensive piece of land, called the Park, which appears as if it *must* have belonged to Beaufort House, but this my informant could not assert; and, on the eastern extremity, Hogmore Lane, dignified for a particular and temporary purpose, into Gloucester Road.

The King's Road divided the Park from the gardens of Beaufort House, and turning towards the river, ran a little way down the west side of them. The Clock House, in my memory, my old chronicler Howard's choice magazine of figs and mulberries raised on a portion of these gardens, is still standing. Below it, and reaching nearly to the Thames, is a row of very moderate houses, which with the gardens of houses built to the east of Lindsey House, circumscribe that very much.

Howard's house was a lodge to the gate of the stable-yard, which gate still remains, and was, when he related this, that of the Moravian buryingground. Stabling within it for 21 horses, was then a school for their sect, so that there has been a blending of the property attached to Beaufort House with that belonging to Lindsey House. I must not omit, that as if to define the boundary of the royal right of way, the print gives, at right angles with the stable-yard gate, a wall, with a gate in it, cutting off the access to the river on the west side of Lindsey House.

But in the print, which allots to Beaufort House its due situation, the centre, there intervenes between the back of Lindsey House and the front of the stables, which are precisely marked by the introduction of horses and grooms, a very respectable mansion, built in the Dutch taste, and of much earlier date, at least in its external, than Lindsey House or Beaufort House. It is cruelly hemmed in; and either that or Lindsey House must have had little or no garden; I should indeed say positively *no* garden, for *my Dutch house* has a door into that before it, and I see no admission for the Lindseys; but I cannot suppose such a mansion, the residence of a Cleopatra of the reign of Charles II. so wanting in the *agremens* of a villa.

Of this intervening mansion I can give no account, unless it be a Buckingham House, Chelsea, which a Duke of Beaufort is said to have bought, and which Mr. Evelyn mentions.

Beaufort House itself, as represented in the print, and in the drawings of it made by Howard, must have been an edifice of no very great style of magnificence, and hardly equal to the great extent of valuable land about it, which, bounded as I have before said, reached in the south-eastern angle to where was afterwards, and may be now, a butcher's shop at the corner of an alley in the street which runs by the river side, called Lombard Street. I must not date from the *church,* for churches may migrate before this is printed.

What I have to tell of this Beaufort House is this, that Strype mentions it as built on the site of one belonging to the Marquis of Winchester, lordtreasurer, in which the wife of the protector, Somerset, lived and died. Howard had heard that it formerly belonged to Lionel Cranfield, Earl of Middlesex, and had himself found a date of the sixteenth century on the leaden pipes. It stood about midway between the river and the King's Road, and had a public highway before the gates. The south-west corner, he said, was an orchard, and if so, my puzzling Dutch house must have given way to it. On each side the entrance from the water-side, there was a porter's lodge, and there were two other lodges about the midway, which closed in a very handsome sweep; the house appears raised a few steps above this circle, which lies within a square of terraces. — The front exhibits a projecting porch in the centre, and is alternately divided into four bay-windows, and eight large casemented windows; the roof has four pediments, each enclosing a window; and a turret with a clock crowns the whole.

Before the year 1737, the house was sold under a decree of the court of Chancery. Sir Hans Sloane, being desirous of purchases in Chelsea, bought it; but when he had got it, did not know what to do with it. He put Howard into it to take care of it, made what he could of the garden, and obliged Howard to account to him for every pennyworth of the produce. Finding it a great incumbrance, he was advised by Howard to make it weather-tight, and wait for a purchaser; but disbursing for the chance of requital was not the habit of Sir Hans, and with the stingey improvidence

which often accompanies a care for money, he let it go sadly out of repair, and then sold it to two men to be taken down. They stripped it of the iron and lead, and entirely broke their contract, by the tenor of which they were to have paid for it by instalments; and they even had the temerity to persist in plundering without payment, bringing a cart at night to take away what they had prepared during the day for removal.

Sir Hans being informed of their proceedings, ordered Howard, who slept alone in the house, to prevent these depredations; but he would allow no force or means for the prevention. It therefore cost the young Quaker some reference to his own sagacity, to devise the means of obeying this arbitrary mandate; he accomplished it by employing two men-to dig very quickly, a deep ditch across the access from the water, the only way by which the property was assailable; this cooled the courage of the marauders, and in the year 1737, Sir Hans commissioned Howard to pull the house down to the ground.

Till within a very few years, the ground remained in a state that might have admitted of ascertaining the site of the house, but buildings have now shut it out from search, and nought remains but the name, Beaufort Row, to tell how it was once honoured.

Of Sir Hans Sloane himself there are still great memorials existing in Chelsea. The buryingground in the King's Road was, I believe, given by him, and to this a curious circumstance belongs, at least remains on oral tradition. It is said that no intention of devoting it to the purpose for which it is used, existed, till on breaking the ground with a view to build on it, the foundation of a church or chapel, and some human bones were discovered; it was then concluded to have been consecrated, and was respected accordingly.

One of his purchases was the palace of Henry VIII., in which the Princess Elizabeth was nursed, and where was a room called, in Howard's memory, Queen Elizabeth's nursery. He thought no part of the original building re-

mained. When the bishops of Winchester quitted Southwark, one end of this palace was given them for a residence; the other end belonged to Lord Cheney, whence the name Cheney Row, and not, as has been very excusably supposed, from the China manufactory which once flourished at Chelsea, and produced most beautiful specimens of porcelain. Lord Cheney was lord of the manor, and his end of the building was called the manor-house.

Though only parts of the same building, these two ends had each a separate court-yard, divided from the other by a wall. Sir Hans purchased the east end; here he resided, and here he died.

How much does remain, and how long any may remain, of that part we have known as the Bishop of Winchester's palace, made part of his see by act of parliament, it is not easy to tell; Sir Hans Sloane's part has long been gone. The grounds extended as far as the whimsical museum, known by the vamped-up style and title of Don Saltero's Coffee-house, and the row of houses westward of *that,* was built after this part of the old house was pulled down.

From this house Sir Hans was buried. Howard was employed in the removal of his books, which amounted to nearly forty thousand volumes; his collection is known to all Europe.

He was, Howard said, a very good landlord, and a very just master, but in no degree liberal, for he gave him no recompense for his accurate plans and measurements of Beaufort House, and though when he engaged him in the superintendence of his purchases, it was agreed that this engagement should not hinder Howard from accepting other employment as a land-surveyor, he never would give him leave of absence.

At one time Sir Hans Sloane used the house higher up the river, now Lady Cremorne's, for a retiring place, and here he would dine on eggs and bacon, or tripe and parsley. The house consisted then of three rooms, one over another; it was built by a man of the name of Pilkington, afterwards occupied by a crazy man, called Captain Kitchin, and from him Sir Hans bought it.

Sir Hans Sloane was the first English physician made a baronet. The rank was conferred on him by George the First on his accession.

I must not revel any longer in Chelsea antiquities. Return we into our track.

My father had two friends, on whom he could rely in any need of a *locum tenens,* as chairman of the quarter-sessions. The one was Mr. Brettell of the Stamp-office, to whom his situation in the West Middlesex militia, on its earliest establishment, gave the title of Colonel. He lived long after Sir J. H., and to an age that gave him another title, " the venerable," with about as much right to it as that which may be brought forward by the heads of some conventual houses. He had been young at a time when few of his own standing thought much of " the days in which there is no pleasure." He had been a *gay man,* as it was then termed, and *a. free liver,* as those were denominated who lay up store of melancholy work for their latter years, and subject themselves to the evil of painful disease on a shattered frame. Of this description of uncurbed spirits, he was, however, one of the best. He had great good sense, and an extensive knowledge of the world, as he found it. He was most honourable in his dealings, most faithful in his friendships, and most liberal wherever his great and accumulating wealth could be useful. But his habits of parsimony were hardly to be surpassed by the Jennings, the Elwes, or the Ransom of any period. He had a town house, which was only to the last degree dirty; but his villa, on one of the most beautiful eminences north of London, was in a condition that would have deterred many from sleeping in it, even in a moderate breeze.

It was said, that he had a sort of money-intercourse with some who appeared his most intimate friends; but this I am not authorised to assert.

I know that he and his lady, who was of a most grotesque appearance, but of the most lively goodhumour, were at perfect ease with persons of peculiar distinction, and whose notice conferred honour; but the Colonel played off his merry mood, and his lady preserved her costume of dirty housewifery, and poured forth her *lomo-descript* volubility, with insensibility to all feelings connected with *mauvaise honte.*

Many knew the shades of Colonel B. 's character — many more, perhaps, than those who knew its brighter tints; and, unfortunately, the circumstances of his last moments did not contribute to his fair fame. He had passed the age of ninety, and had been some time confined to his bed: a violent cough attended his gout, and a spasmodic fit of this disturbing concomitant seizing him while giving orders to his coachman for the payment of bills, he expired with a canvas bag of cash in one hand, and a *rouleau* of bank-notes in the other. It was a study for a moral painter; but the Colonel's very fine features, and waving silver locks, which gave him credit wherever he appeared, would ill have accorded with the character to be represented.

Of his lady, no one can say that *shades* obscured *her* character; it was all a uniform sunshine of high spirits, which was not seldom rather oppressive to persons of reflection; but as these spirits made her an excellent wife, an entertaining travelling companion, and served to support her to the last under a direful disease, they were to be regarded as a blessing. Had her epitaph been a record of her tone of mind, I think the question, "What does it signify?" would have been read on her tombstone.

The other associate, on whom my father could rely, was the well-known Saunders Welch, a man of obscure origin, but inheriting some property in the county of Buckingham. He was what would now be called a police-magistrate, and was at the head of an office, in which certain magistrates sat in rotation. He was in person, mind, and manners, most perfectly a gentleman, and when the dinner dress required the bag, the sword, and *chapeau bras,* and the clothes were frequently decorated with gold or silver, I used to open my eyes very wide to see Mr. Welch, and some others of my father's intimate friends, *even now living,* enter the drawing-room.

Mr. W.'s tastes led him to literature of rather a grave cast, probably, tinged by the early loss of a very amiable wife; and he had a love for the arts and the professors of them, and for foreigners and persons of diffusive knowledge, which had procured for him a very enviable situation in society. His wife had left him with two girls, the eldest still in the nursery. Carrying pride and prejudice a little beyond the grave, she had extorted from him a promise never to marry again; an engagement tantamount to a systematic rejection of that which might be of the greatest possible benefit to her children, if prudently done. He had religiously, but against his judgment and inclination, kept his promise, and had lived a life of blameless morality among men not of the most sober habits. I do not recollect that I ever saw him laugh; but he was cheerful, and had much to tell of men whose follies he viewed with mild regret.

Of the symmetry of Mr. Welch's person, an idea maybe conveyed, by recording the fact that Roubilliac modelled from his leg and foot for the statue of Handel, which was, and probably may still be in Vauxhall Gardens, and of which my father used to remark, that the praise of most of the beholders was bestowed on the slipper, which hung negligently on the foot.

Experience shows that this preference of *tri/ling to important* excellence is common; but what will be said to a lady of some pretensions in society, and who had resided at Rome, who in a comparison of painting with sculpture declared the latter was more agreeable to her, because "it took a better polish?"

In noticing the aptitude of the ignorant, to seize on the minor parts of excellence, I must record the astuteness of a sailor, who gazing on a ship, the name and head of which were the Queen, muttered that it was the king's concubine, and not the queen, for she had no wedding ring on her finger. I had this from our old friend Captain Gostling, of the artillery, of whom I have more to say.

I wish I could recall more than one

anecdote of his; but that one I will give to the best of my recollection. He had known much of Henry Fielding, and heard him, even when his fortunes were very desperate, promote some thoughtless frolic of extravagance, by saying that he never in his life knew the difference between sixpence and a shilling Peter Walter, who was then of great notoriety as one of the most successful money-getters in London, hearing him utter this sentiment, replied gravely, "A time will come when you *voill* know it." "When?" said Fielding. "When you are worth only eighteen-pence," replied Peter.

It is consentaneous with our best feelings, and encouraging to the exertions of our fellow-creatures, to admit that the competition for the best situations in our favoured country, is, with as few exceptions as good order can allow, open to all; and it is remembered as one of the liberal axioms of George III., that "no British subject is by necessity excluded from the peerage." Consistently with this sentiment it was, that he checked a man of high rank, who lamented that a very good speaker in the court of Aldermen, was of a mean trade, by saying with his characteristic quickness, "Pooh, pooh! What signifies a man's trade?—A man of any honest trade may make himself respectable if he will!" Whether an anecdote which I had from Mr. Thrale's friend, Mr. Evans, of St. Olave's, Southwark, be new to the reader, I cannot form an opinion: for the correctness of it, I will answer, as far as regards Mr. E. Henry Fielding, hearing from a friend that a third person was very much dejected, asked the cause. "Because," said his friend, "he is deeply in debt." "Is that all?" replied the facetious Harry; "you surprise me, that he should mind it. How happy should *I* be, could I find means to get 500*l*. deeper in debt than I am 1" I confess I am often surprised at the jealous caprice with which we ladies view what we call the encroachments of the classes below us on our prescriptive rights to distinction. We have made no scruple, of late years, of a sort of masquerade adoption of low fashions, and an imitation of those

whom the necessity of hard labour or of braying bad weather compels to wear suitable clothes. It is almost folly to record fashions, which a very short time will render obsolete, but I shall always be intelligible if I quote the introduction of a market-woman's scarlet cloth cloak at the opera; the mob cap of a fish-woman, and absolutely named the Billingsgate, worn with jewels; morning dresses, and even not morning, made of woollen which, by the fire, gives out the strong smell of the oil in which it has been prepared. To all these there ever must be standing objections; and I know not how it could be made consistent with the critical *costume* of the house of Kemble, when Mrs. Siddons drest Queen Katharine, who must at the time of her divorce have been about thirty-seven years of age, in an old woman's cap and a regal diadem. Katharine was a Spaniard, and, with the advantages of her national dress, would have made a deeper impression and proved her tyrant still more unjust.

But the caprice of adoption is little, compared to that of deprecation. Our *own soubrettes* may be as fine as they choose to be, but the presumption of any one who can do *us* no credit, is stigmatised without the smallest analysis: and, utterly ignorant of the impudent slatternly finery of tradesmen's daughters, and servants half a century ago, even neatness, if it sets off a pretty person, is reproved. I have heard an old servant in our family say that in her youth she never dressed without a hoop; and at even this, perhaps no Dutch woman would wonder. But the worst forgetfulness is of the peculiar pretensions of

This was certainly proved in the case of Saunders Welch, who, early in life obtaining credit for the good use he had made of opportunities to acquire knowledge and improve the powers of his mind, lived to see his house the resort of persons distinguished in the elegant arts, and the *belles lettres*. He had indeed recommended himself to the government, at a time when factious attempts were the mercantile world, to the enjoyment of its wealth. We have no

merchants now, indeed, who make fires of cinnamon, and kindle them with royal bonds, but we have those whose high credit and extensive correspondences, even without other pretensions, contribute to support the fabric of the monarchy, and to carry into effect the counsels of the legislative power. These, surely, may enjoy unenvied their massy side-boards and their costly cellars, and, in their hospitable use of the good things of this world, spread wide the honour of their country, and make others strike their flag to its navy with abated reluctance.

Again, we have another description of commercial men not rising so high in the scale of wealth, but who, by the union of talents with industry, connect themselves with men of all honourable descriptions. And not only in England, but in Ireland, now rising to every eminence of distinction, are these to be found. I know well a firm in Dublin, the partners of which, though engaged in an extensive manufacturing concern, are men of the most elegant pursuits; distinguished as much by attention to business, by uniform civility and suavity of manners as by their mechanical knowledge.

making to shake the throne, under the plea of chastising ministers, by his intrepidity in restraining a mob assembled for the *noble* purpose of destroying the wall before Bedford House, a wall of singular beauty and elegance which extended on the north side of Bloomsbury Square from east to west, and the gates of which were decorated with those lovely monsters, sphinxes, very finely carved in stone. Between this wall and the mansion, was a spacious court-yard, far better harmonising with the rank of such a dwelling, than the under-ground area and paltry railing of the fashionable residences of the present day.

The house itself was a long, low, white edifice, kept, in the old Duke's time, in the nicest state of good order, and admirably in unison with the snowwhite livery of the family. It had noble apartments and a spacious garden, which opened to the fields; and the uninterrupted freedom of air, between thisjsituation and the distant hills, gave it the advantages of an excellent town-house, and a suburban villa.

But to return, the claim which Saunders Welch had on the confidence of government, or the gratitude of the well-disposed, would have done little for him in a drawing-room *conversazione:* on the contrary, his situation as a magistrate of the metropolis, would, under the then existing policemanagement, have been in his disfavour. But away from business, he was not only the associate of men of genius, but, in some instances, their patron; and, at times, a contributor of a light essay to the periodical effusions of his day.

He was left with two infant daughters; and his promise to his wife precluding him from doing what might have been best for them, they were reared I know not how, and educated in an awkward desultory way. The elder was beautiful, so beautiful as to prompt the Marquis of Rockingham to say, when she was married to an artist, " We shall now know from whom you copy Venus;" the younger, as remarkably plain: and I may now venture to say what I could not say in another place where I have described the younger, that the disparity in intellect was equal to that in person, but happily in the inverse ratio.

Neither of the young ladies, I must confess, had a fair chance for what is called success in life. When taken from a nurse, I believe they had an antiquated *gouvernante, 'a* French woman of the old school, who managed the one very ill and the other not at all. The beauty was, after some experimental plans, put under the care of Mrs. Lennox, a lady of too eccentric a genius to render any service to a young person of less than moderate intellect and whose ideas were bounded by the fashions of dress, in which it must be confessed she made a figure of distinguished elegance when she had returned home, and took her place at the head of her father's house. When the sun of youth was rather declining, she was bestowed on Nollekens, the sculptor, who, though of power in his art to charm into forgetful-

ness of *himself,* was not a husband for such a woman. But her father was anxious for her settlement; and I can conceive that on the blank page of such a mind it would have been difficult to find characters expressive of approval or disapprobation. Whether the prospect of white satin and fine laces, pale pinks, pale blues, lilacs, and jessamines, might not connect itself with that of a house "of one's own," I will not say; but this I can affirm, that it was not till the parties had very much disagreed, that any idea of compulsion on the part of the father got abroad.

Marriage made a great alteration in the lady. She, who for many years had dieted herself, solely, and almost confessedly, "for her shape," on vegetables, and that meagre beverage called "Imperial," immediately gave up all solicitude for her person. She astonished us all, by coming out into a bulk, that made one's heart ache for the penance in whalebone which she must have endured. She had sat to the elegant artist of the day, Mrs. Kauffinan, better known by her name of "Angelica," and had been exquisitely painted, with a dove pecking at her ring; it was a beautiful picture, a likeness and not unfairly flattered, and must hand down the artist and her subject to posterity, as showing a most fortunate meeting,—excellence in portrait-painting, with a subject on which its peculiar style could be best exercised.

But who would have known the "sitter" for this portrait, when, before its colours were well hardened, she apologised for, or rather justified, the most negligent appearance, by saying, in the tone of Johnson, which by being much in his company she had acquired, that it was of little consequence, at " her time of life," whether she was two or three inches bigger or less.

I had seen her in her bridal *costume,* when, as was the fashion of the day, "she received company;" and lovely she was, even, when compared with the wife of Mr. Paradise, and a Greek lady, of a singular style of beauty, who accompanied her. But never, never after, did a trace revive of what she had been. Her dress became very fantastic; I for-

get whether it was the *pastoral* or the *picturesque* that she affected — it might be the one or the other for any resemblance that was obvious — but she professed her taste, and owned her imitation.

She had attempted to attain something of the show of a power of thinking; and what she said, she accompanied with a gentle action, of her hands. She had occasionally been abroad, and by her husband's situation was led into the world of the arts; but instruction, when poured on her mind, ran off it as from polished marble, and with every advantage, she to the last remained sadly illiterate; and dejection taking the vacant seat of vivacity, she sunk lower and lower in importance.

It may, however, raise the lady in the public estimation, if I say of her, as I can on the testimony of her sister, that she is the original of Johnson's Pekuah in Rasselas. If the intimate attention of such a man was an honour, she consequently had much to boast of, and indeed he treated both the ladies as he might have done nieces.

Excessively offended at her sister's having joined the Romish communion—a defection I cannot palliate, but on which the wife of a Roman Catholic should have been moderate—she yet urged the privilege of that church, when, at the age of about forty, not having received the rite of confirmation, she took advantage of it to change her name from Mary, which was her mother's, to Maria, with which she had no connection!

Whether any memoir of Nollekens has appeared, or will appear, I know not — but were it candid and circumstantial, it might be amusing to those who do not refine too much.

Every thing belonging to his exterior appearance, conversation, and slovenly manners, was at variance with his ideas, for surely he has been rarely equalled in the branch of art which he professed. If I may be allowed to give an opinion, he was inferior to the deceased Bacon in group The just appreciation which men of real talent form of the works of their rivals, and the modest opinion they maintain of their own performances, are the strongest proofs of abilities greater than those which their works testify. But yet there is a species of what appears at first sight *pride,* which has its origin in a much better feeling. I shall not injure the memory of West, if I say that I think he had this. He has stood with me before a picture in his study, pointing out its merits, and endeavouring to excite my astonishment at the rapidity with which he had painted it; but I believe this arose from a comparison of what he had achieved, with his own expectations from himself, and an exultation at having done so much. It is not a sign of the truest modesty to say, "O! bless your soul! this is nothing to what I *can* do."

Bacon was always discontented, Nollekens seemed unconscious of difficulty — it was all mechanical in his eye, and he would spend his evenings in looking over engravings, etchings, and drawings, with an admiration showing that he thought real excellence was to be found, not in what *he* could do, but what these imperfectly recorded. I have heard those say, who have seen him modelling, or partaken of the dust and fragments flying about his head as he worked, that the ease with which he produced the effect, would almost have tempted them to say, "Give *me* too a bit of clay," or "lend *me* the chisel."

In Bacon's estimation, the Duke of Argyll's monument in Westminster Abbey stood very high; I remember his telling my father that he could find no fault in it, but that it had the ing, but in a single figure unrivalled by any contemporary. His Venus chiding Cupid, his Venus taking off her sandal, his statue of Pitt, his busts, must commit his memory to posterity, as a sculptor of the first taste.

But a more stupid, good-humoured man in company, never sure could be found to complete a dinner-party, than the owner of these fine ideas. It name of Roubilliac to it, instead of that of Bacon. He said of his own performances of this kind, that he always endeavoured to convey some moral sentiment — something that should excite reflection; and

certainly he often fulfilled his purpose admirably. His designs even for a clock-case will show this. He executed one for the Queen's palace, which he decorated with a cock on one side, and an aloe on the other. Vigilance and Patience were thus recommended.

I flatter myself that he was not at liberty when he graced a tablet to the memory of a maiden lady, who lived beyond the age of seventy, with the lovely figures of Peace and Innocence. Allowing every probable sort and degree of merit to the party, surely there are emblems of character better suited to the age of threescore and ten, than those, which few of us could challenge as not forfeited even in early life.

A short time before his death he was applied to, to design and execute an idol for a temple in the East Indies. He told my father he was beginning to think on the subject, when the recollection struck on his mind, that it would be contrary to the letter of the second commandment: he instantly gave up.

I wish I could recollect the many stories I have heard of Roubilliac. is told of him, that, presenting a picture of his own painting in the Royal Academy, he was required to explain his meaning in some parts. The subject was Abraham entertaining the Angels; and he began to discourse on his mode of treating his subject, in rather a puzzling manner, concluding abruptly with, "You see they are saying, how d'ye do, Abraham, like." The cognomen of "Abraham-like" stuck to him for some years of his youth.

When contracting for the monument for Pitt, it was necessary to hint to him, that even at his then time of life, the chances were against his living to complete it, he was therefore desired to name the artist on whom the task should devolve. Chantrey had not then come forward: he said without hesitation " Westmacott." In naming this fine artist, I cannot forbear inserting an anecdote, perhaps, indeed, not told here for the first time, which shows his power of captivating the affections. When his exquisite statue of little Lady Lucy Russel was exhibiting at Somerset Place, a la-

dy, who had just come from it, called to a little boy whom she had before been leading by the hand, to follow her, but he continued to loiter. She spoke again and I heard him reply in a sort of short breathing — " Mamma, mamma, I can't get away from it."

As far as I was capable of observing, he was a man of no conversation, excepting on his art, and very imperfectly on that; and with such a wife, he did not improve in temper or manners. They kept separate purses. Her fortune had been settled on her for her own use; and, as there was no child, there was no common interest or feeling. It became a strife of sordidness. He made her keep the house at her own expense; and disputes were frequently resorted to for ascertaining what did, and what did *not,* come within this description of expenditure. She valued herself on the integrity of her ceconomy, and justly; for, in a doubt whether a friend or two would accept an invitation to "stay and dine," the guest has overheard an order to the cook, "Don't make the pudding till the last minute, for, perhaps, they won't stay." An order surely better whispered.

Under such sordid ceconomy, the human Dr. Johnson gave her, on her marriage, some of his best advice, and honoured my mother still more by advising an imitation of her domestic ceconomy, the liberality of her table, and the scrupulous neatness of her person. Had I judged by the resemblance of the copy to the original, I should have supposed his advice had been understood as irony.

mind must be in a state of progressive ruin. I do not wish to drain to the lees such sour mixtures. This man of fine ideas sunk into a sad state. He had survived his wife; and curiosity has been excited to know how his wealth, which must be very great, has been disposed of. With this I have no concern; but I remember Mrs. Welch's uniform supposition that it would go to Rome. He had sums for his works, which I dare not, on the sole evidence of my memory, set down, but I know that he had one hundred guineas each for as many busts of

Mr. Pitt.

Mr. Welch's other daughter remains to be spoken of, and though I have elsewhere taken pains and pleasure in delineating her character, I shall here speak of her more largely, and with the conscientious view of inculcating on young women, disposed to enjoy to excess that which is good only when moderately pursued, the moral obligation of paying attention to the practical duties of a female.

I have said that the two motherless girls were for a short time reared at home, under the same casual discipline, but I have heard Mrs. Welch, as she latterly styled herself, speak of being at one period of her childhood, at some one of the great schools of the time, and I suppose a school of some distinction, as she remembered Lady Elizabeth Percy, the daughter of the then Earl and Countess of Northumberland, a fellow-disciple. *She* recollected being sent from home by the *gouvernante*, in a style either of novelty or oddity, and the girls all assembling round her, and calling to each other, "Come and look at little Nanny — she's all French."

What she attained here, I know not, but certainly it was time she should go somewhere, as she had even then begun to argue on the uselessness of things having names, if they were not to be called by them.

Somehow she learnt drawing — somehow she learnt music, on the fashionable instrument, the guitar—and somehow she learnt seven languages, and made a considerable proficiency in the mathematics. Thus instructed, she fell into the literary society of her father's house, and while her sister addressed herself to the ladies of those who were family-men, "little Nanny" cultivated the friendship, and enjoyed the intimate conversation of Johnson, and his friends, Charlotte Lennox, Baretti, Paradise, Sir Joshua Reynolds, the family of Mr-Wilton, and many others of the first colloquial talents of the time. With Angelica Kauffman , Wilson f, and many other artists, she was at home: and, improving in herself all her father's tastes, had she been at all vain,

she might have held a distinguished place in the class of literary ladies contemporary with herself. Mrs. Piozzi, Angelica, as she was called, resided with her father in Golden Square, and held very agreeable Sunday-evening *conversaziones*. I have heard it said, that she was addressed by a painter of the first eminence,—I do not like to name him,—it was not Sir Joshua; — she refused him, and, in cruel revenge, he dressed up a smart fellow, of a low description, but some talent. This man, he introduced to her as a foreigner of distinction, and teaching him to profess a passion for her, his specious recommendations deceived her, and she married him. They parted immediately. — I wish the story may not be true.

t I remember to have heard her quote many of Wilson's expressions, in viewing subjects for his pencil. A sky he characterised as "pingible," or not so; — and when she had built her house at Ardenham Hill, near Aylesbury, she conceived a great dislike to the trees on the opposite rising ground of Winchenden, which were thinly and formally planted, recollecting Wilson's antipathy to what he called "Asparagus beds.' whose recitals want that first ingredient, accuracy , and whose conduct through life proclaimed a sad I am justified in saying that Mrs. Piozzi is inaccurate, by the testimony of the Reverend Mr. Evans, who, having the living of St. Olave's, Tooley Street, was frequently a guest at her table. In reading her representation of facts, as they occurred under his own knowledge, and her report of things said in his hearing, he declared against the fidelity of both; and when reduced to fact, it was often observable, certainly to the credit of her invention but at the expense of her correctness, that the worth of a tale, or the wit of a repartee was furnished by herself.

I should call Mrs. Thrale, as she was when known in the world, and Mrs. Welch, exactly the contrast of each other; but I know not at what period I could contrast them; for Mrs. T. was as much a contrast to herself as to any one else. I have heard a servant, who was taken from her family into my mother's nurs-

ery, describe her as a very odd lady, who condescended to the cares, and even below the usual cares, of a notable housewife. From Johnson's reproofs and petulant censures of her, it is to be inferred that she, at times, varied her *costume* greatly; and whenever I have seen her, it was very much under the similitude of a Frenchwoman a little indebted to her own hands for her roses.

That she was most liberally endowed with a luminous mind, in itself an invaluable blessing, I recollect with admiration. I have heard from old Lady Lucy Meyrick, that at five years of age, travelling in Wales, and seeing the date on some very ancient building, she, without hesitation, and without any calculation, named the number of elapsed years.

The following is a genuine anecdote. After the death of Mr. Thrale, a friend of Mr. H. Thornton, canvassed the borough, with a view to Mr. H. T.'s representing it in parlia want of judgment, has said of her, that "with every mean of being agreeable, she had not the power ment. He waited on Mrs. Thrale, who took pains to be of service. She concluded her obliging expressions with saying, "I wish your friend success; and I think he will have it: he may probably come in for two parliaments, but if he tries for a third, were he an angel from heaven, the people of Southwark would cry,' Not *this* man, but Barabbas.'"

Before I record another fact respecting this eccentric lady, I must insist on the reader's considering the peculiar irritation under which the letter referred to was written, and that the exceptionable words may be taken in their primitive sense: —

I was deeply occupied with my father in the examination and selection of Dr. Johnson's papers, and can truly say, that the tenderest regard was shown to the feelings of every individual. There was a great accumulation of letters: one of them was the reply to that in which Johnson had severely reprehended her second marriage. It contained an eulogium on the object of her choice: his profession was ranked as in itself very high, and his excellence in it was said to be acknowledged in places of the highest repute for taste. But the most remarkable words were these: "My second husband is a gentleman, which is more than could be said of my first. " Taken in common acceptation, these words are reprehensible, but taken literally, inasmuch as a profession constitutes gentility and a trade does *not,* Mrs. P. is correct: the sound of the words is worse than the sense. But there is a humorous terseness in the reply, that makes it curious; and the more logical the head that had to decide on them, the more evident their truth. It was I who discovered the letter: I carried it to my father: he enclosed it and sent it to her, there never having been any intercourse between them.

of being so." This is hardly fair: she could not certainly have recommended herself as Mrs. P. did, of whom I have heard it said, that into whatever company she fell, she could be the most agreeable person in it; but neither would she have resorted to Mrs. P.'s methods of pleasing.

But she pleased once in a way rather inconvenient. Her father had a very good man-servant, of rather a superior class in understanding. Without complaint or apparent discontent on either side, he on a sudden very respectfully desired to be discharged. Of course, some reason was asked for by his master. He replied, "that Miss Anne's conversation at table was so delightful, that he could attend to nothing else; that he was deeply in love with his young mistress, and for that reason solely, thought it best to quit his place."

It must have been a mind of a peculiar cast in that rank of life, that could be gratified by her mode of thinking and speaking. Her tones, from living much with Johnson, had acquired a modulation unlike that of other females. She did not, indeed, as I have heard it said Mrs. Thrale did, imitate his pomposity of diction; but, except when the tenderness of her feelings was excited, her recitative was not pleasant; and the argument which she had used in her infancy, operated on her mind when an adult. She gave what she thought the

proper names to things; if *we* spoke of *dress, she* called it *apparel;* she talked of *esculents, anAfood,* and *provisions,* when we spoke of *eatables* and *victuals s money* was *coin,* an *account-book* was a *diary of expenses; servants* were *domestics,* the higher class *attendants.* These were blemishes, but blemishes that subtracted little from the sterling worth of her character. Witty attempts were made to render her ridiculous; but it is much easier to caricature, than to imitate that which approaches to excellence. She never designed to be singular, or affected to be superior; if she was the former, it was the result of an awkward education, if the latter, it was because she had received from the hand of her Creator a strong and virtuous impulse to make the most of his gifts and of her time. Accustomed as she was to society, she seemed to hesitate in speaking, as soon as she found herself heard with attention. When obliged once, by a request from my father, to repeat a few lines of a Latin hymn used in the Romish church, she was distressed, and though then forty years of age, excused her embarrassment by saying, that she had never before uttered so many Latin words. And in a conversation, where the un-oppressive Bennet Langton was one, she suffered an argument founded in error to pass, for want of courage to correct it.

Her anecdotes of those with whom she had lived would have been valuable, but I believe she made it a point of moral duty never to commit to paper, lest her father's pride and partiality might induce him to bring forward what she wrote. I know that this fear prevented her from keeping any journal whilst abroad: her diffidence at that time, when the publication of tours, even in the nearest countries, was rare, might be regretted; as, besides occasional residences in French Flanders and the French vicinity, she had been obliged to resort to the climate of the South of France to save her life, after a visit to the Peak, in which she had paid dearly for the pleasure of exploring. On her return to England, she remarked, that the air of Montpelier resembled more that

of one of our windy days in March, than what it was described to be; an opinion, which, till within a very few years, nobody seems to have entertained. I have repeatedly heard Twickenham called the Montpelier of England, and we have our Montpelier Row, which stands with its face to the *east.* Mr. Hughes, in his brilliant Itinerary, describes Montpelier as standing on an elevated plain, bleak and exposed. The late exemplary Countess of Waldegrave told me, that till she reached Nice, she found no benefit from change. Lord Byron found none of the fine Ausonian temperature short of Athens; and we now hear it confessed, that our own south is preferable to any part of Europe.

Her natural quietness of temper made her a cool spectator of many circumstances that would have implicated others. Her intimacy with Charlotte Lennox, who, though one of Johnson's favourites, was, I think, as little entitled to favour as most women, afforded her opportunity of observing with a contemplative eye, obliquities which to many would have been intolerable. When residing with her sister in the house of Mrs. Lennox, notwithstanding the want of all order and method, all decorum of appearance, and regularity of proceeding, she endeavoured to extract from the mind of her hostess what was good, and smiled at all the rest. But it must have been a *dernier ressoii* to place her, or any female, in a family thus illordered, and with a woman whom I saw in a court of justice fairly pitted against a low female servant, who had endeavoured to obtain a compensation for ill words and hard blows received from her mistress. Mrs. Lennox made a compact with Baretti for mutual assistance in learning each other's native language; but Baretti complained that she fell far short in her part of the treaty. It concluded with a quarrel. He once, in company, bestowed more of his notice on her little girl than she approved, and desiring him to desist, and not to let that child engross his attention; she was answered by his saying, "You are a child in stature and a child in understanding." What the measure of the latter was I do not know, but her translation of Sully's Memoirs shows, that however it ended, it began in a praxis on rendering the language, for nothing can be much worse translated that the first pages of it; and I have heard it said, that, in translating Brumoy's Greek Theatre, she rendered *les enfans perdus* by " the lost children."

Baretti, I suppose, was generally provoking, where opportunity offered. He carried this power to such excess once, at an evening visit at Mr. Paradise's, as to excite Mrs. Paradise, who was little less irascible, to defend herself by turning the scalding water of the tea-urn on him.

Mrs. Paradise was remarkable for possessing a mind and person totally at variance. Nothing could be more elegant or refined than her whole exterior; her countenance was indeed unquiet, but her voice was gentle, and her manner deliberate. At the head of her table, with a large dinner-party, perceiving that a plate before her was not quite clean, she beckoned the servant, and said to him in an audible whisper, —" If you bring me a dirty plate again, I will break your head with it." At a practice of dancing, in which her daughters were to bear a part, one of them not pleasing her in her performance, she rose, came forward, and giving her a box on the ear that made her reel, she returned to her seat in the most undisturbed silence.

My younger brother remembers to have met Mrs. Paradise one day at dinner at Mrs. Welch's; her personal attractions were at that time much on the decline, and her countenance retained little other expression but that of extreme irritability. She then resided at one of the villages in the neighbourhood of London, and regretting that there was no stage-coach from her village, which would convey her to that part of London to which her business occasionally called her, he suggested that the deficiency might be supplied by availing herself of another conveyance, to take her to her place of destination, when she quitted the stage. Upon which, turning to him, with a most emphatical look and tone of voice, she said, "Lord! Sir, you

might as well advise me- cut off my nose to improve my face." My brother was astonished, and could not perceive any connection between the two propositions.

I never was so surprised as by hearing my father say one morning, when he had just dismissed two visitors from his study, that they were Mr. Langton and Mr. Paradise, who had come to consult him on the *elopement* of Mrs. Paradise. Mr. Langton, I confess, was apt, "constitutionally, to take many things too seriously; and this was one. The *elopement* was nothing more than Mrs. Paradise's withdrawing with one of her daughters, because she could not make Mr. P. consent to a match for her, which she approved, as leading into high rank in a foreign land. She married her daughter as she wished — and she then returned: the hue and cry was absurd.

Mr. Paradise was a man, I believe, meriting better treatment. He was a Greek; his wife, I forgot to say, was a strenuous American republican. Mr. P. had an extensive intercourse with foreigners; and persons of the first class were recommended to his introduction. In a morning-call, he told my father that he was just come from visiting a young Russian of very high rank, who was travelling through England. He had lodged him at what was then Lowe's Hotel, in Covent Garden, the elevated situation of which had afforded him a fine view of the sports of a mob, whose amusement was the tossing and catching a

The tendency of one recollected fact to introduce not only its relatives, but those with whom it has no cognisable connection, makes me seek for a memorandum which I owe to our friend the Chamberlain of London, and which he gives me on his own accurate knowledge.

There was to be met in the literary society of London, about the year 1779, at Sir Joseph Banks's, Mr. Hastings's, Mr. Hoole's, and houses of such elegant reception, a native of Jerusalem, of the name of Telamas, whose father had been a dragoman at Constantinople. He himself was an Asiatic of the finest

race; and had been sent hither with over-land despatches, from Lord Pigot, at Madras. He spoke English with scarcely any imperfection. In his dress he adopted a style combining the Turkish costume, with that of this country. He was a man.of thought and reflec dead cat. The young man had been attentive to the scene as characteristic of the country: he remarked on the difference between this and the metropolis of his own, in which, he said, had such a crowd assembled, a military force would soon have been in sight to disperse them.

tion; and he had made reading the eight volumes of Buffon's Natural History, the Amusement of a Passage to India.

While in the East Indies, he was swimming across a river, when he saw a tyger spring up on the opposite shore. He swam back: the tyger followed. His party on the shore prepared to shoot the animal, yet feared wounding Telamas: but the tiger making a spring out of the water, as if to dart on the unhappy man when he should reach the shore, they aimed and were successful!

He had passed through Macedonia, and attentively observed the people. He said that what he saw of them, convinced him of the perfect credibility of what we read of Alexander.

In the Great Desert, he had once been overtaken by a heavy rain. Thoroughly wet and weary, he had at night reached a place of shelter, but into which he was refused admittance. It was not only full, but full of persons infected with the plague. The *danger* he set at nought; he said he must die of fatigue if not of disease: he was therefore suffered to lie down in his clothes, in the only vacant place in a long gallery. The man near whom he had placed himself, was a corpse the next morning, but Telamas escaped uninfected.

While the two daughters of Mr. Welch remained together, the younger was little sensible of the deficiency of her general knowledge; but when in the decline of life, he was advised to try a foreign air, and would take only his younger daughter with him, she felt bitter regret at her ignorance of common things; and I have heard her, with tears in her eyes, recommend to young women the use of the needle, and some knowledge of the preparation of food. I suppose the inconvenience she felt, might have stimulated her to assume a character, in which such acquirements could not be expected; but it was not pleasant to her friends, when Humphrey, the crayonpainter, brought intelligence of having met her in Italy *en garfon.*

The want of attention to matters which she had thought of small importance, was very perceptible after the death of her father, on whom she had most piously attended. She was the *second* person in her small establishment. She never could learn the art of providing; and, in her dress, she depended entirely on the taste and good sense of a common servant. On all subjects she reasoned "high;" and it would have been difficult to convince her, that a good dinner yesterday, was not as fit a dinner for today.

Left very much by her father to choose the church to which she should attach herself, she was too open to the representations made to her, when in Rome, of the superiority of that communion from which the Church of England had diverged. She adopted it, and remained in it, though its austerities were extremely at variance with her health; and when visiting her, I have been grieved and vexed to see her uncomfortable meal on *jour maigre*

Having built herself a house near Aylesbury, in Though I would on no account resist or teach resistance to the authority under which it is our happiness to live, I could not deny the truth of a country foot-boy's reasoning, when compelled to observe a public fast, by not dining till close of day. "I am sure," said he, "we should not have thought half so much about eating, if we had got bur dinners, as we do on common days, at one o'clock."

Buckinghamshire, purely because she thought it right to settle herself amongst some dependent relations, she made her garden her first object, and became an erudite botanist. In London, as she advanced in life, and her health declined, she supplied the loss of evening-engagements, by applying herself to conchology, and became a referee in the science.

Very much accustomed to the society of Johnson, she had imbibed his spirit of silent meditation, and when her mind returned again to its flow, she seemed as if she had resorted to some one to consult. Without affecting to *study* any thing—for I never heard her mention the now hackneyed term "studies"—she had a fair, firm opinion to bring forward on most subjects, and she had acquired an axiomatic diction which, with its attendant circumstances of voice and gesture, made what she said well remembered. In the outset of life, when first at liberty to act for myself, I was much indebted to her for many useful precepts. One was to learn to rely on my own judgment, rather than to ask advice. She said, that with all possible explanation, it was hardly practicable to put another person in as intimate possession of facts as was necessary to a right judgment. But particularly she objected to seeking advice from two persons; as, in case of disagreement, it must throw the decision back on ourselves, whether we were, or were not aware of it.

She was sometimes supposed to *imitate* him; but I believe any resemblance was no more imitation, than that which gives the Scotch or Irish tone to the voice of persons living amongst those people. Lady Rothes, who was a native of Suffolk, was a strong instance of this perfect but unintentional acquirement. Mrs. Piozzi, when living much with Johnson, had his tones, which sat very ill on her little French person. After her second marriage she had lost them. I once heard a lady, who, I think, never could have seen Johnson, speak so entirely in his manner, that she made me start.— Mad dogs were the rage just then in the neighbourhood; and the reports of them seemed to make them as many as the reporters. "I do not believe all this," said this lady: "it cannot *rain* mad dogs." The terseness of the reply, and I may add its *effect,* were as strong resemblances of Dr. Johnson as the tone.

Referring to that neglected school, the school of experience, she, without pretending to take an interest in politics, understood well the affairs of the world. In the first irruptions of the French, she set at nought the notion of the ease with which they might be crushed. She had Caesar's Commentaries in her mind, and the Gauls in her recollection.

In calling to mind what can be recovered of this extraordinary and excellent woman, who would now be far more justly appreciated than when she lived, I am assisted by my brother, to whom she gave as a reason for applying to Greek, that learning the grammar was an employment in itself so little attractive, that it left her mind perfectly willing to be called off by the attentions her father's state of health then required.

She had never, I think, learnt any thing, beyond what was imposed on her under tutelage, but on the best of all impulses,— the want of the knowledge in her power to attain.

Notwithstanding her turn of mind, she obliged herself to a certain degree of personal attention; and said, that during her father's illness, feeling no *motive* to change her dress before dinner, she argued backwards, and made the want of motive, the motive itself, for fear that a habit of negligence should grow on her, and make her appearance dejecting to her father.

She used to blame extremely that want of foresight or inclination which made persons, particularly parents, in questions of reasonable indulgence to their children, averse from "meeting expense." It was a situation in which she" was never to be found, even while building her house. And this she proved in a most friendly manner on the death of my father, when she hastened to us with the offer of a considerable sum of money, then lying at her banker's, in case the forms of law should restrain us from using our own. We felt the kindness as much as if we had needed it— and equally were we indebted to her delicacy, in driving to our house with all the manisfestation of urgent business, lest the sight of a carriage at the door might draw upon us unseasonable calls.

Nor would she quit London, though at a beautiful season, till she had seen us settled under this great change.

She used to remark on the great difference between the body of accumulated and original thought observable in Johnson, while his circumstances compelled him to solitude, and the loose texture of his mind when incessantly pouring out in society. The same degree, but not the same sort of difference, was remarkable in herself; but the advantage was in the contrary scale. Her sister was no companion to her, nor was she even a hearer; and in truth, when they met to pass a day, Mrs. Welch generally put a book into her sister's hand to keep her quiet—not from any want of affection, for she was most tenderly attached to her. And when absent from us in the country, unless by good fortune some person of an accomplished mind came near her orbit, her thoughts were confined to herself; but they were not restrained by any undervaluation of others. All her neighbours had her true neighbourly love, and their virtues had her due estimation. Indeed, her description of them, rather gave them, than robbed them of importance. But when she returned to her London friends, and their society, she was for a time what we used to call *foggy* or *smoky.* As soon as the abundant fuel of her mind was well kindled, it then burnt clear and brilliant; and at the end of a friendly day, she was as fresh and as unwilling to cut the thread of conversation, as she could be at any period of the time.

She made, however, no exertions to relieve herself from solitude, when the presence of a friend was almost indispensably necessary during her last illness; but submitted in the gentlest way to all the privations of decay. Having no power to amuse herself, and having settled herself in one of the clean but perfectly still situations in Bath, the watching some sparrows on an opposite roof, became interesting to her, and kept her in a sort of vacant observation, precluding all collection of ideas.

I was with her in her last hours, as much as her lamentable adoption of another faith permitted; and a melancholy scene did I witness. Her sister shrunk from the task, but the most humane and judicious kindness was afforded by ladies at Bath, where she ended her days: they were strangers to her, but before I could reach her, had made it forgotten that they were so. But friendship could do nothing for her: the physician and apothecary were in attendance; the priest was in the, room with them, and was waiting till she could be prevailed on to submit to the rites of the church, in the bosom of which she had spent many years. I could not insert any thing so ludicrous as the conduct of her personal servant, were it not in itself another argu

Her reluctance was great, and her sturdy tone of refusal was nearly of the pitch of Johnson's; nor till the power of opposition failed, would she submit. What a lesson it was! A lesson that taught me how far preferable it was to grow up contentedly, and to decay gradually, under the easy yoke and light burden of the church, out of whose pale she had suffered herself to be argued.

I now come fairly to speak of Johnson, who belongs to every period of my father's life; but here I must of necessity disappoint the reader. My father has told all that I know; and what I myself observed is not worth detailing. I can therefore only speak of circumstances respecting him as they occurred.
ment in favour of more regular proceeding. The woman had lived several years with her, and was deemed trustworthy j and on this occasion, though very ignorant, was employed to persuade her to submit to that which she could not explain. I had left the chamber, impressed with the persuasion that I should see her no more, but calling the next morning, and hearing she was still alive, I desired to see her servant. To my astonishment and horror, I saw the creature in a state of intoxication; and to *my* enquiries she thus replied: " Oh, ma'am! I have had such a night! At three o'clock my poor mistress called out, 'How d'ye do, S—?' and I said, 'Pretty well thank you, ma'am.' Oh, such a night!"
When first I remember him, I used to see him sometimes at a little distance from the house, coming to call on my father; his look directed downwards, or rather in such apparent abstraction as to have *no* direction. His walk was heavy, but he got on at a great rate, his left arm always fixed across his breast, so as to bring the hand under his chin, and he walked wide, as if to support his weight. Getting out of a hackneycoach, which had. set him down in Fleet Street, my brother Henry says, he made his way up Bolt Court in the zigzag direction of a flash of lightning, submitting his cpurse only to the deflections imposed by the impossibility of going further to right or left.

His clothes hung loose, and the pocket on the right hand swung violently, the lining of his coat being always visible. I can now call to mind his brown hand, his metal sleeve-buttons, and my surprise at seeing him with plain wristbands, when all gentlemen wore ruffles; his coat-sleeve being very wide, showed his linen almost to his elbow. His wig in common was cut and bushy; if by chance he had one that had been drest in separate curls, it gave him a disagreeable look, not suited to his years or character.

I certainly had no idea that this same Dr. Johnson, whom I thought rather a disgraceful visitor at our house, and who was never mentioned by ladies but with a smile , was to be one day an honour, not only to us but to his country.

My ignorance was suited to my powers of judging; but how, after Johnson's death, George Keate, whose evanescent little wit is now obsolete, could take upon himself to prophesy that Dr. Johnson's fame would be short-lived, I know not. This he did in a conversation with Sir J. H., at Nicol's, the bookseller's, in Pall Mall.

I have been reproved for speaking coolly of Johnson, when the zeal for his character was most I remember a tailor's bringing his pattern-book to my brothers, and pointing out a purple, such as no one else wore, as the doctor's usual choice. We all shouted with astonishment, at hearing that Polypheme, as, shame to say! we had nicknamed him, ever *had* a new coat; but the tailor assured us he was a good customer. After this I took notice, and, *ex pede Herculem,* concluded from what remained visible, that the coat had been originally of this fugitive colour.

fervid; but a high authority has said, "a prophet is never without honour, but in his own country;" and in this, to say nothing of our Divine Teacher's spiritual knowledge of the heart of man, is declared the nature of things. What is near us, is seen in petty detail — what is removed, we behold in the grand aggregate; the mountain, contemplated only as we pass over it, gives little idea of its sublimity; it is from the distant valley we must see it, to feel awed by its thousand feet of height, and its miles of extent. There was nothing in Johnson's exterior to impress — and I had not been taught to admire what I could not comprehend, and which no grace of manner recommended; on the contrary, I should soon have been ridiculed out of any affectation of "discovering talents." Nor could I, at any time, catch from my father any of that spirit of adulation which was subsequently excited in the breasts of those who foresaw that it would be creditable to have been of Johnson's acquaintance. My father judged of him as of his I can conceive nothing much more ridiculous or less in harmony with the manner in which I was, I will not say *edu*other friends, but certainly appreciated him most highly. I remember the eagerness with which he purchased and read his Idler and his Scotch Tour; but the former, I think, disappointed him. In the latter, he seemed to recognise all the comprehensiveness of his mind, and the turgid compression of his style. And in his political pamphlets he admired him, and unwillingly was he driven to confess, even to us his children, that Johnson could ever have written on principles opposite to those which he afterwards adopted. It appears now, indeed, little less than virtue to have been what was called a Jacobite; and certainly there was no small degree of virtue, and of many virtues, in the adherence to a royal cause, more perhaps than *could* be practised on the other side; but still it

would *cated,* but *broke,* to the drudgery of my father's pursuits, than the idea of a presentation to " the illustrious Dr. Johnson," or the being set to write a " pretty letter" to him for the sake of getting a reply. Had I succeeded, I am sure ray mother would have burnt it, lest it should make me vain, as I have seen her serve Dr. Reynolds's visiting ticket of enquiry after a long attendance on me; and I am not certain that Johnson, with all his regard for my father, might not have concluded the perusal of my pretty penmanship, as he received a bevy of damsels, with "Fiddle de dee, *my* dear. " be a hardy champion who would venture to defend the two parts of Johnson's conduct, and a subtle sophist who could reconcile his opinions. The answer of a sensible woman of rank, when reproached with marrying beneath herself, "My dear friend, one would do a,great deal for a good home," is perhaps the best that can be suggested for Johnson. He made good use of the comfort he had gained; and though, as in the case of Archbishop Seeker, no one can commend the means by which the power was attained, yet if, as in his case, it was well used, we must be content, and take human nature as we find it.

My father, in the Life of Johnson, speaks of his well-known determination, never to reply to any attack made on his political writings, and quotes, as the basis of this resolution, Bentley's aphorism, that "no man was ever written down, but by himself." He, however, confesses, that in the instance of one reply to The False Alarm, he was disposed to defend himself, but that consulting "his friends, he was advised to forbear."

Why my father should have stated the fact thus vaguely, I cannot conjecture; for I certainly remember, and as clearly as if it had occurred only yesterday, a note coming from Johnson, which requiring an answer, Lady H. sent to Hicks's Hall, where Sir J. was then sitting. My mother had unlimited permission to open all my father's letters; and well she merited this confidence; for I have heard him often say to her honour, that she never betrayed a matter which

he wished unrevealed, or said incautiously one word that he could have wished suppressed.

She was immediately sensible of the importance of this query, which my father alone could answer: she dismissed Johnson's man, and ordered the servant whom she sent, to wait his master's orders. Sir J. wrote from the bench; and thence his reply was sent to Johnson. If my memory does not deceive me, my father showed me the note, for I was of *a very proper age* to be of his privy council, being ten years old! But of his dissuasion and its bearing on Johnson's mind I am confident, though my father has forborne to claim the act as his.

I have occasionally seen a note of Johnson's, beginning in the third person, and ending in the first. To those who know the abstraction, the appearance of *inattention,* which attends excessive *attention,* this will not appear extraordinary.

In Johnson's visits at my father's, the conversation which I heard, had little interest for *me* ,. but I knew by habit— and my ear always expected it— that whatever was brought forward as settled opinion by another, would be met by him with doubt, introduced with "Why, Sir, I see no reason," or, "Sir, if you mean to say," which doubt, after the encouragement of a few more words, became stiff denial or contradiction, and exploded in one of those concentrating periods, which were certainly the peculiar *forte* of his powerful mind.

I can give an instance of his manner, and in a case where possibly he was right. My youngest brother being sent to him by my father on some message, in weather extremely severe, and having heard from our French master, that some distilled scented waters had frozen, repeated this to him as a proof of the intensity of the frost. Johnson said, the waters must have been bad. Henry, in the simplicity of a school-boy, as if to take their part, replied, that it had occurred at Prince Caramanico's. "Then, Sir," said Johnson, "it can't be true—so your story falls to the ground."

I think it might be remarked of Johnson, that persons, rather than things, furnished the subjects of his conversation:

his early life, pitiable as it was, could afford none that would bear repetition: in recollecting friendships and friends, there was a puerile attempt at playfulness, not far removed from the humour of Falstaff, but not sitting so well on the professor of ethics, as on the greasy voluptuary. It was Bozzy and Goldy, and Langty and Hawkey, amongst his intimates.

Of this deviation from the style of manly intercourse, which perhaps was an effort of factitious cheerfulness, I think I may venture to say he would have been ashamed, had my father remarked it to him. The basis of this supposition is his uniform silence on whatever appeared below the level of *their* original intercourse. Boswell's influence over him, came upon us like the discovered power of a mistress; and even the luxuries of Streatham were spoken of by him as the indulgences of an invalid. But when, having lost these, he condescended to society and accepted invitations not in any way doing him credit, I heard my father speak to him of these resources with a tone of gentle reproach: he acquiesced in his opinion, but said, 'I go any where to be at ease; they let me do as I like."

The persons to whom I allude were such as could make no pretensions to his notice, but through the medium of affluence. They had not the claims of his friend Strahan, nor could they draw together the society of Mr. Thrale's table; but, sick at heart, and burdened with a painful existence, he betook himself, like a stricken deer, to any pasture where the sun warmed him, and the herbage was sweet.

The effect on his mind, produced by his almost constant residence at Streatham, was subject of reflection and conversation to Mrs. Welch and my father. No one knew Johnson better than she did, and she uniformly lamented that friction of his mind which mixed company produced, and which they agreed, tended to assimilate him with other men, and consequently, in a great measure abated the originality of his native character.

Whoever compares the style of his

Lives of the Poets with that of his Rambler and his Rasselas, will, I think, perceive this. I never can read a page of the Lives without feeling fatigue, and having in my mind's eye the attempts of a tired post-horse to be expeditious; and, on the contrary, never do I see the postilion's arm raised beyond the usual angle, and feel the threatened animal trying for a few seconds to mend his pace, but I think of the Lives of the Poets. The feeling is involuntary, and therefore, I hope, will be forgiven.

None of Johnson's friends, I think I may say, except those who formed the parties at Streatham, liked or could approve his engrossing engagements there. "We never can see him, if we call," "He is never at leisure, if we invite him," were sentences I often heard; and till the idle employment of writing the Lives of the Poets was found for him, The author of a very witty fiction, written, I believe, with a good intention, but some profligacy, has characterised Blair's Sermons as written in "little asthmatic periods." On this my fancy may have founded itself.
a task which he made deserving of himself, only by indulging in the see-saw of wayward criticism, his mind was running to waste in the small coinage of a populous home.

Others might merely lament this monopoly — many would have sought the opportunity of selfintroduction. My father was indignant; but this feeling was not deep; he remembered what Johnson had been, and as eagerly caught at opportunities of hearing of him, as a brother would have done under a separation, on *his* part painful.

On the death of Mr. Thrale, it was concluded by some, that he would marry the widow, — by others, that he would entirely take up his residence in her house, which, resembling the situation of many other learned men, would have been nothing extraordinary or censurable. The path he would pursue was not evident, when on a sudden he came out again, and sought my father with kind eagerness. Calls were exchanged; he would now take his tea with us; and in one of these evening visits, which

were the pleasantest periods of my knowledge of him, saying, when taking leave, that he was leaving London, Lady H. said, "I suppose you are going to Bath." "Why should you suppose so?" said he. "Because," said my mother, "I hear Mrs. Thrale is gone there." "/ know nothing of Mrs. Thrale," he roared out; "good evening to you." The state of affairs was soon made known.

It is greatly to the honour of Johnson, that he never accustomed himself "to descant" on the ingratitude of mankind, or to comment on the many causes he had to think harshly of the world. He said once to my youngest brother, "I hate a complainer;" this hatred might preserve him from the habit: whether, indeed, it was possible for *any habit of speech* to consist with that of " talking for victory," which he professed, and which certainly made him dependent on the tenet of his adversary, I cannot judge.

Of his charities, or the claims on his feelings, I believe he never spoke. On many points, he talked with so little settledness of opinion, that it was difficult to adjust the worth of any thing by it. I heard him say that my father's Walton's ComF plete Angler, was the best edited book in our language. I love the book, but I could as soon swallow *it,* as this extravagant compliment, which, in the nature of the work, cannot be true; and I would pledge myself that had Steevens, or Boswell, or Davies, the next day, in their whispered spleen, remarked on it as ill done, Johnson would have replied, "Why, if Hawkins liked the book, Hawkins had a right to indulge in writing notes on it, but if the book afforded little matter for them, little is to be expected from them." In this way I heard him take the part of Sir Matthew Hale, saying, " If Hale had any thing to say, let Hale say it;" a species of, I do not know what to call this mode of framing a sentence, to which he was very prone. His *Jiat,* however, was certainly on the right side, if the importance of Sir Matthew Hale's writings be considered.

The club at the Turk's Head Tavern, in Gerrard Street, was, in my earliest recollection, a I do not wish to prolong the memory of what is not in itself respectable; but in a witty but profane song, there is a line on this plan, that seems a caricature of Johnson's manner.

"For Habbakuk's cold had made Habbakuk hoarse." source of great pleasure to my father; and I am sure he regarded his own secession as a painful, but perhaps it might be a fancied, necessity. It has been invidiously commented on, and even I myself must own that the reason he has assigned is short of satisfactory. In my own mind I am convinced, however he might persuade himself, that he was disgusted with the overbearing deportment of Burke, and his monopoly of the conversation, which made all the other members, excepting his antagonist, Johnson, merely his auditors. My father used often to quote that passage in one of the quaint productions of Herbert, the author of "The Country Parson," —

"A civil guest
Will no more talk all, than eat all the feast."

He was not himself impatient of listening; and it was his rule, and one which he expected others to observe, never unnecessarily to interrupt a speaker; but, that Burke's practice was not as forbearing, I have heard Mr. Langton complain very seriously. "The Burkes," as the men of that family were called, were not then what they were afterwards considered, nor what the head of them deserved to be considered for his splendid talents; they were, as my father termed them, "Irish adventurers," and came into this country with no good auguries, nor any very decided principles of action. They had to talk their way in the world that was to furnish their means of living; and it could not be expected that they would lay down their tools to witness the prowess of those who had less stimulating motives. But this intolerance did not recommend them to favour; and, perhaps, part of that which the luminary of their house obtained in the club, was owing to the amusement afforded by the conflict of eloquence, when Johnson was excited into argument.

Nothing could recommend itself less

to the favour of Sir J. Hawkins, than what was said of Mr. Burke, That this obtrusive disposition in the Burke family, was not notional, nor the too quick perception of a fastidious mind, may be proved by Johnson's own expressions, particularly with regard to the extolled son of Edmund Burke; of whose disrespectful deportment towards himself, Johnson complained to Mrs. Williams; and it would be very false and unjust modesty in me, if I did not add that he contrasted it strongly with the respectful behaviour of my brothers.

on his coming forward. It was known that Lord Rockingham, however good his intentions, was a weak man, and glad to avail himself, at some expense, of the talents of those who could support his administration. That Mr. Burke stood first among these, all I have heard leads me to suppose; and my father soon perceived that he meant to offer himself to the highest bidder. He mentioned this opinion to Johnson, who not only concurred in it, but said that he believed Burke meant so to be understood. *Loquitur H. H.)* Of Burke, however, it may be truly said, that if any man were calculated to claim universal attention, it was he. His stupendous variety *of* knowledge, his command of language, his taste, his power of expressing the finest ideas that could enter the mind of any human being, rendered him, in the opinion of all who could appreciate his excellence, and, among the rest, of Johnson himself, the first man of the time in which he lived; and as long as eloquence will charm, his works will hold a place amongst the most valuable productions of human genius."

If I may be allowed to prove Johnson's respect and esteem for my father, from his having acted clandestinely by him, I should quote the secrecy with which he established the "Essex Street Club," in 1783, exactly one year before his death, and after he had held the most serious conversations with him on the most important subjects, and had talked on the fitness of abstraction from the world. I remember, after this shadow of conviviality had been got up, his inviting my father and mother to spend an evening

with him, and positively on "club-night:" and I never shall forget one of his adulators calling in, in his way to this right honourably designated meeting, "just," as he said, " to have the pleasure of informing the club of the state of his health." Johnson listened as he might have done to a deputation from the cats; and got rid of the enquiry to resume his conversation on the irritability of Warburton, and the better spirit of Sir Matthew Hale. I remember his speaking with great emphasis of the value set by the latter on the leisure necessary to acquaintance with ourselves, and of his regret on the obstructions his legal situations had put in his way.

When Johnson spoke with tenderness, uncouth as were his gesticulations, and distorted as were his features, the interest he expressed was affecting. Particularly I recollect hearing him repeat the lines concluding Izaak Walton's Life of Bishop Sanderson, with a fervour that impressed them at once on my memory.

In endeavouring to correct errors, I will not suffer myself to depart from the strictest demands of truth. Boswell was well justified in his resentment of my father's designation of this same Essex-Head Club, as a sixpenny-club, meeting at an ale-house; for in what respect was it inferior to that which he formed in 1749, at a beef steak house in Ivy Lane? The rate of admission could be no consideration in a society to which neither wealth nor rank could introduce; and whatever it was as a *house,* Johnson's presence would have absolved it from indignity. Perhaps it was, of eligible places, the nearest to his residence, and, therefore, gave the best chance for his ability to meet his friends. As to "a presidency in rotation," the fable of " the Lion and other beasts hunting" solves every difficulty. Woe had betided the president who should presume to preside when Johnson was there. I am sorry my father suffered himself to seem pettish on the subject: honestly speaking, I dare say he did not like being passed over, and I am sure he never construed Johnson's secrecy as I do. It is my fault that the passage stood; had

I said to him what I do here, it would have been struck out of the manuscript. Turning over "The Life," to ascertain a fact, I am vexed at a passage that admits of two constructions. It relates to Jarvis's Don Quixote. That Jarvis had not ability to proceed far with it, and that Tonson put it into the hands of the Reverend Mr. Broughton, reader at the Temple Church, is, I dare say, correct; but he is said to have acquired in a few months, "*as was pretended,* sufficient knowledge of the original to give a translation in the true spirit of the author." Now, whether the period of time, or the *truth of the spirit,* be the *pretended* circumstance I know not; but had I, when I was copying "The Life" for the press, known the extraordinary fidelity and beauty of what is called Jarvis's translation, I certainly should have asked the removal of this qualifying expression. This translation, Smith's Thucydides, and Farnworth's Davila, are the best translated works I ever read; and I cannot doubt that the Guicciardini of Farnworth is as good. In the Davila, I recollect only one misapprehension; and with regard to the translation of Cervantes, it is to be wished, that it had been applauded as it deserves, in order to rescue the English reader from the *travestie* of Smollet, which is disgraceful and disgusting. Our opinion of translations

There is a point of Johnson's character, little, I think, insisted on, at least not so much applauded as it claims to be. He was, with all his infirmities bodily and mental, less of the thorough-bred *irritabile genus* of authors, than most of his compeers; he had no petty feelings of animosity to be traced only to mean causes. He said of some one indeed, that he was "a good hater," as if he approved the feeling; but I understand by the expression, that it was at least a justifiable, an honest and avowed aversion, that obtained this character for its possessor. As for Johnson himself, pity must have interposed between him and censure, had he been the *sncfrler* of his time, if his causes of discontent be considered. He could not, for any space of time sufficient to correct the

natural failing of our nature, remain as a child ignorant of his superiority over his should be formed on collation, and such a test would show how often we are cheated where we have implicit confidence. I did not believe old Giannini, when he told me that Hoole, in his Tasso, had omitted the difficult passages; but it is true in most instances.

Fs playfellows and competitors; he might as well be supposed to have remained ignorant of his gigantic frame. As soon, therefore, as he was, if I may so say, warm in his own approbation, he must have begun to feel the obstacles of his inborn infirmities; he was made for ponderous strength, but not for agility, or even muscular activity; he found himself with a defective sight, and very soon the dreadful disorder which might have paralysed his powers, at the moment when he became sensible to the possession of them, showed itself with great violence, and, perhaps, by the resistance it met in the toughness of his ligaments, was turned on his mind and spirits. Whatever uneasy feeling this produced, instead of being opposed more and more effectually, as he advanced to middle life, was rendered more and more annoying by the necessity of exertions which required ease of body and freedom of thought. And this increase of uneasiness it was that drove him to the sad experiment of seeking medical opinion. This being awfully unfavourable, his fate seemed fixed, and he was doomed *to* a deplorable conflict, without certainty of averting the dreaded evil. All his greatness was now so much against him. The lion in toils could not be expected to submit like that proverbial image, the lamb; and it is not consistent with our present state to suffer thus, without a reflecting look on ourselves, and a comparison with others.

Under such grievous circumstances, every effort was doubly meritorious, every failure was entitled to a larger measure of compassion, and every forbearance of enry and jealousy was, I trust, of higher value in the sight of Heaven.

But still more to his honour is it, that

his irritability was not excited by the most common cause of mortification. He saw the companion of his studies, and the witness of his poverty, Taylor, raised by the tide of human affairs to bloating affluence, and, I should presume, with pretensions of every kind, far, very far inferior to his; yet I do not recollect having ever heard of a sigh excited by this disparity of lot. That he envied Garrick, while he loved and admired him, is true and well known; but, it was under the pardonable feeling of jealousy in seeing histrionic excellence so *d* much more highly prized than that which he knew himself to possess. Goldsmith he laughed at, and called him an idiot, but it was " an inspired idiot;" and no feeling in his mind would have prevented his rendering him such assistance as would have purchased him more fame, and even without claiming the credit of it.

To Warburton's great powers he did full justice. He did not always, my brother says, agree with him in his notions, "but," said he, "with all his errors, *Si non errasset, fecerat ilk minus."*

Speaking of Warburton's contemptuous treatment of some one who presumed to differ from him, I heard him repeat with such glee the coarse expressions in which he had vented this feeling, that there could be no doubt of his hearty approbation. It is therefore another point of merit, if, as I believe is the fact, Johnson never descended to scurrility. Some of what are called the *Variorum* Classics might be brought forward to prove what language the learned of Europe have thought befitting scholars. Sad, sad waste of time, paper, and labour, and defeating the very purpose it is used for, by increasing the bulk and price of their volumes.

It will relieve the monotony of my own observations, and show how one of Johnson's best and most intimate friends, understood his feelings towards Garrick, if I here insert the admirable imitation of his style and manner, which Sir Joshua Reynolds threw on paper, without any intention of its ever seeing the light. I owe the communication of it to a lady, whose uncle was one of Johnson's friends, and who lived herself in great intimacy with Sir Joshua's family. As it was once surreptitiously introduced into a magazine, but at a time when far less likely to attract attention than at a latej period, I avail myself without scruple of the permission given me, with every acknowledgment of the favour done to me, and to my readers, if I have any.

The following *jeu d?esprit* was written by Sir Joshua Reynolds to illustrate a remark which he had made, "That Johnson considered Garrick as his property, and would never suffer any one to praise or abuse him but himself." In the first of these supposed dialogues, Sir Joshua himself, by high encomiums on Garrick, is represented as drawing down upon him Johnson's censure: in the second, Mr. Gibbon, by taking the opposite side, calls forth his praise.

JOHNSON *against* GARRICK.

Dr. Johnson *and* Sir Joshua Reynolds.

R. Let me alone, I'll bring him out. *(Aside.)* I have been thinking, Dr. Johnson, this morning, on a matter that has puzzled me very much; it is a subject that I dare say has often passed in your thoughts; and though / cannot, I dare say *you* have made up your mind on it. *J.* Folly, folly! What is all this preparation? What is all this mighty matter? *R.* Why, it is a very weighty matter. The subject I have been tlunking on is this, Predestination and Free-will; two things I cannot reconcile together, for the life of me. In my opinion, Dr. Johnson, Free-will and Foreknowledge cannot be reconciled. *J.* Sir, it is not of very great importance what *your* opinion is upon such a question. *R.* But I meant only, Dr. Johnson, to know *your* opinion. *J.* No, Sir, you meant no such thing: you meant only to show these gentlemen that you are not the man they took you to be, but that you think of high matters sometimes; and that you may have the credit of having it said, that you held an argument with Sam. Johnson on Predestination and Free-will: a subject of that magnitude as to have engaged the attention of the world, and to have perplexed the wisdom of man for these 2000 years; a subject on which the

fallen angels, who had not yet lost all their original brightness, found themselves in wandering mazes lost. That such a subject could be discussed in the levity of convivial conversation, is a degree of absurdity beyond what is easily conceivable. *R.* It is so, as you say, to be sure: I talked once to our friend Garrick upon this subject; but I remember we could make nothing of it. *J.* Oh, noble pair! *R.* Garrick was a clever fellow, Dr. Johnson. Garrick, take him altogether, was certainly a very great man. *J.* Garrick, Sir, may be a great man in *your* opinion, as far as I know, but he was not so in *mine:* little things are great to little men. *R.* I have heard you say, Dr. Johnson,— *J.* Sir, you never heard me say that David Garrick was a great man; you may have heard me say that Garrick was a good repeater of other men's words—words put into his mouth by other men: this makes but a faint approach towards being a great man. *R.* But take Garrick upon the whole, now, in regard to conversation. *J.* Well, Sir, in regard to conversation; I never discovered, in the conversation of David Garrick, any intellectual energy, any wide grasp of thought, any extensive comprehension of mind, or that he possessed any of those powers to which *great* could with any degree of propriety be applied. *R.* But still — *J.* Hold, Sir; I have not done. There are, to be sure, in the laxity of colloquial speech, various kinds of greatness; a man may be a great tobacconist; a man may be a great painter; he may be likewise a great mimic: now you may be the one, and Garrick the other, and yet neither of you be a great man. *R.* But, Dr. Johnson, — *J.* Hold, Sir; I have often lamented how dangerous it is to investigate and to discriminate characters to men who have no discriminative powers. *R.* But Garrick, as a companion, I heard you say no longer ago than last Wednesday at Mr. Thrale's table,— *J.* You tease me, Sir. Whatever you may have heard me say no longer ago than last Wednesday at Mr. Thrale's table, I tell you I do not say so now: besides, as I said before, you may not have understood me, you misapprehended me, you may not have

heard me. *R.* I am sure I heard you. *J.* Besides, besides, Sir, besides, do you not know, are you so ignorant as not to know, that it is the highest degree of rudeness to quote a man against himself? *R.* But if you differ from yourself, and give one opinion to day, — *J.* Have done, Sir. The company, you see, are tired as well as myself. T'OTHER SIDE.

Dr. Johnson *and* Mr. Gibbon.

J. No, Sir; Garrick's fame was prodigious, not only in England but over all Europe: even in Russia, I have been told, he was a proverb; when any one had repeated well, he was called a second Garrick. *G.* I think he had full as much reputation as he deserved. *J.* I do not pretend to know, Sir, what your meaning may be by saying he had as much reputation as he deserved; he deserved much and he had much. *G.* Why surely, Dr. Johnson, his merit was in small things only: he had none of those qualities that make a really great man. *J.* Sir, I as little understand what your meaning may be, when you speak of the qualities that make a great man: it is a vague term. Garrick was no common man: a man above the common size of man may surely, without any great impropriety, be called a great man. In my opinion, he has very reasonably fulfilled the prophecy which he, once reminded me of having made to his mother, when she asked me, how little David went on at school, that I should say to her, that he would come to be hanged, or come to be a great man. No, Sir; it is undoubtedly true that the same qualities united with virtue or vice, make a hero or a rogue, a great general or a highwayman. Now Garrick, we are sure, was never hanged, and in regard to his being a great man, you must take the whole man together. It must be considered in how many things Garrick excelled, in which every man desires to excel: setting aside his excellence as an actor, in which he is acknowledged to be unrivalled; as a man, as a poet, as a convivial companion, you will find few his equals, and none his superior. As a man, he was kind, friendly, benevolent, and generous.

G. Of Garrick's generosity I never

heard: I understood his character to be totally the reverse, and that he was reckoned to love money.

J. That he loved money, nobody will dispute; who does not? But if you mean by loving money that he was parsimonious to a fault, Sir, you have been misinformed. To Foote, and such scoundrels, who circulated those reports; to such profligate spendthrifts, prudence is meanness, and ceconomy avarice. That Garrick in early youth was brought up in strict habits of ceconomy, I believe; and that they were necessary, I have heard from himself: to suppose that Garrick might inadvertently act from this habit, and be saving in small things, can be no wonder. But let it be remembered, at the same time, that if he was frugal by habit, he was liberal from principle; that when he acted from reflection, he did what his fortune enabled him to do, and what was expected from such a fortune. I remember no instance of David's parsimony but once, when he stopt Mrs. Woffington from replenishing the teapot; it was already, he said, as red as blood; and this instance is doubtful, and happened many years ago. In the latter part of his life, I observed no blameable parsimony in David: his table was elegant, and even splendid; his house, both in town and country, his equipage, and, I think, all his habits of life, were such as might be expected from a man who had acquired great riches. In regard to his generosity, which you seem to question, I shall only say, there is no man to whom I would apply with more confidence of success, for the loan of 200*l.* to assist a common friend, than to David; and this too with very little, if any probability of its being repaid.

G. You were going to say something of him as a writer, you don't rate him very high as a poet.

J. Sir, a man may be a respectable poet without being a Homer, as a man may be a good player without being a Garrick. In the lighter kinds of poetry, in the appendages of the drama, he was, *if not* the first, in the very first class. He had a readiness and facility, a dexterity of mind that appeared extraordinary even to men of experience, and who are not apt to wonder from ignorance. Writing prologues, epilogues, epigrams, he said he considered as his trade; and he was what a man should be, always and at all times ready at his trade. He required two hours for a prologue or epilogue, and five minutes for an epigram. Once, at Burke's table, the company proposed a subject,,and Garrick furnished his epigram within the time; the same experiment was repeated in the garden, and with the same success. *G.* Garrick had some flippancy of parts, to be sure, and was brisk and lively in company, and by the help of mimicry and story-telling, made himself a pleasant companion; but here the whole world gave the superiority to Foote, and Garrick himself appears to have felt as if his genius was rebuked by the superior powers of Foote. It has been often observed, that Garrick never dared to enter into competition with him, but was content to act an under part to bring Foote out. *J.* That this conduct of Garrick's might be interpreted by the gross minds of Foote and his friends, as if he was afraid to encounter him, I can easily imagine. Of the natural superiority of Garrick over Foote, this conduct is an instance; he disdained entering into competition with such a fellow, and made him the buffoon of the company, or as you may say, brought him out. And what was at last brought out, but coarse jests and vulgar merriment, indecency, and impiety, a relation of events which, upon the face of them, could never have happened, characters grossly conceived and as coarsely represented? Foote was even no mimic, he went out of himself, it is true, but without going into another man; he was excelled by Garrick even in this, which is considered as Foote'a greatest excellence. Garrick, besides his exact imitation of the voice and gesture of his original, to a degree of refinement of which Foote had no conception, exhibited the mind and mode of thinking of the person imitated. Besides, Garrick confined his powers within the limits of decency; he had a character to preserve, Foote had none. By Foote's buffoonery and broad-faced merriment, private friendship, public decency, and every thing estimable amongst men, were trod under foot. We all know the difference of their reception in the world. No man, however high in rank or literature, but was proud to know Garrick, and was glad to have him at his table; no man ever considered or treated Garrick as a player: he may be said to have stepped out of his own rank into a higher, and by raising himself, he raised the rank of his profession. At a convivial table, his exhilarating powers were unrivalled, he was lively, entertaining, quick in discerning the ridicule of life, and as ready in representing it, and on graver subjects there were few topics in which he could not bear a part. It is injurious to the character of Garrick to be named in the same breath with Foote. That Foote was admitted sometimes into good company (to do the man what credit I can) I will allow, but then it was merely to play tricks. Foote's merriment was that of a buiFoon, and Garrick's that of a gentleman. *G.* I have been told, on the contrary, that Garrick, in company, had not the easy manner of a gentleman. *J.* Sir, I don't know what you have been told, or what your ideas may be, of the manners of a gentleman. Garrick had no vulgarity in his manners; it is true Garrick had not the airiness of a fop, nor did he assume an affected indifference to what was passing: he did not lounge from the table to the window, and from thence to the fire; or whilst you were addressing your discourse to him, turn from you, and talk to his next neighbour, or give any indication that he was tired of his company; if such manners form your ideas of a a fine gentleman, Garrick certainly had them not. *G.* I mean that Garrick was more overawed by the presence of the great, and more obsequious to rank than Foote, who considered himself as their equal, and treated them with the same familiarity as they treated each other? *J.* He did so, and what did the fellow get by it? The grossness of his mind prevented him from seeing that this familiurity was merely suffered, as they would play with a dog; he got no ground by affecting to call peers by their surnames;

the foolish fellow fancied that lowering *them* was raising himself to their level. This affectation of familiarity with the great, this childish ambition of momentary exaltation, obtained by the neglect of those ceremonies which custom has established as the barriers between one order of society and another, only showed his folly and meanness; he did not see that by encroaching on others' dignity, he put himself in their power, either to be repelled with helpless indignity, or endured by clemency and condescension. Garrick, by paying due respect to rank, respected himself. What he

G gave was returned, and what was returned he kept for ever; his advancement was on firm ground; he was recognised in public, as well as respected in private, and as no man was ever more courted and better received by the public, so no man was ever less spoiled by its flattery. Garrick continued advancing to the last, till he had acquired every advantage that high birth or title could bestow, except the precedence of going into a room; but when he was there, he was treated with as much attention as the first man at the table. It is to the credit of Garrick, that he never laid any claim to this distinction; it was as voluntarily allowed as if it had been his birth-right. In this, I confess, I looked on David with some degree of envy, not so much for the respect he received, as for the manner of its being acquired. What fell into his lap unsought, I have been forced to claim. I began the world by fighting my way. There was something about me that invited insult, or at least a disposition to neglect, and I was equally disposed to repel insult, and to claim attention, and I fear continue too much in this disposition now it is no longer necessary. I receive at present as much favour as I have a right to expect; I am not one of the complainers of the neglect of merit.

G. Your pretensions, Dr. Johnson, nobody will dispute; I cannot place Garrick on the same footing; your reputation will continue increasing after your death: when Garrick will be totally forgot, you will be for ever considered as a classic.

J. Enough, Sir, enough: the company would be better pleased to see us quarrel than bandying compliments.

G. But you must allow, Dr. Johnson, that Garrick was too much a slave to fame, or rather to the mean ambition of living with the great, terribly afraid of making himself cheap, even with *them,* by which he debarred himself of much pleasant society. Employing so much attention, and so much management upon such little things, implies, I think, a little mind. It was observed by his friend Colman, that he never went into company but with a plot how to get out of it; he was every minute called out, and went off or returned as there was or was not, a probability of his shining. J. In regard to his mean ambition, as you call it, of living with the great, what was the boast of Pope, and is every man's wish, can be no reproach to Garrick; he who says he despises it, knows he lies. That Garrick husbanded his fame, the fame which he had justly acquired both at the theatre and at the table, is not denied; but where is the blame, either in the one or the other, of leaving as little as he could to chance? Besides, Sir, consider what you have said: you first deny Garrick's pretensions to fame, and then accuse him of too great attention to preserve what he never possessed.

G. I don't understand — J. Sir, I can't help that.

G. Well but, Dr. Johnson, you will not vindicate him in his over and above attention to his fame, his inordinate desire to exhibit himself to new men, like a coquette ever seeking after new conquests, to the total neglect of old friends and admirers.

"He threw off his friends like a huntsman his pack," always looking out for new game.

J. When you quoted the line from Goldsmith, you ought in fairness to have given what followed,—

"He knew when he pleased he could whistle them back;" which implies at least that he possessed a power over other men's minds approaching to fascination. But consider, Sir, what is to be done: here is a man whom every other man desired to know; Garrick could not receive and cultivate all, according to each man's conception of his own value: we are all apt enough to consider ourselves as possessing a right to be excepted from the common crowd. Besides, Sir, I do not see why that should be imputed to him as a crime which we all so irresistibly feel and practise c we all make a greater exertion in the presence of new men than old acquaintance. It is undoubtedly true that Garrick divided his attention among so many, that but little was left to the share of any individual; like the extension and dissipation of waters into dew, there was not quantity united sufficiently to quench any man's thirst: but this is the inevitable state of things; Garrick, no more than another man, could unite what are in their natures incompatible.

G. But Garrick not only was excluded by this means from real friendship, but accused of treating those whom he called friends, with insincerity and double dealing. J. Sir, it is not true: his character in that respect is misunderstood. Garrick was, to be sure, very ready in promising, but he intended at the time to fulfil his promise; he intended no deceit: his politeness or his good nature, call it which you will, made him unwilling to deny; he wanted the courage to say *no,* even to unreasonable demands. This was the great error of his life: by raising expectations which he did not, perhaps could not, gratify, he made many enemies; at the same time, it must be remembered that this error proceeded from the same cause which produced many of his virtues. Friendships, from warmth of temper too suddenly taken up, and too violent to continue, ended, as they are like to do, in disappointment; enmity succeeded disappointment: his friends became his enemies; and those having been fostered in his bosom, well knew his sensibility to reproach; and they took care that he should be amply supplied with such bitter potions as they were capable of administering: their impotent efforts he ought to have despised, but he felt them, nor did he affect insensibility.

G. And that sensibility probably shortened his life.

. *J.* No, Sir, he died of a disorder of which you or any other man may die, without being killed by too much sensibility. *G.* But you will allow, however, that this sensibility, those fine feelings, made him the great actor he was. *J.* This is all cant, fit only for kitchen-wenches and chambermaids. Garrick's trade was to represent passion, not to feel it. Ask Reynolds whether he felt the distress of Count Hugolino when he drew it.

G. But surely he feels the passion at the moment he is representing it.

J. About as much as Punch feels. That Garrick himself gave into this foppery of feelings, 1 can easily believe, but he knew at the same time that he lied. He might think it right, as far as I know, to have what fools imagined he ought to have; but "it is amazing that any one should be so ignorant as to think that an actor will risk his reputation by depending on the feelings that shall be excited in the presence of two hundred people, on the repetition of certain words which he has repeated two hundred times before, in what actors call their study. No, Sir, Garrick leftnothing to chance; every gesture, every expression of countenance, and variation of voice, was settled in his closet before he set his foot upon the stage.

It is impossible to read even this burlesque of manner without adverting to the truths accidentally contained in it, which are entirely consonant with the ideas of Diderot in a little tract I have heretofore mentioned as existing in Baron Grimm's miscellaneous correspondence. Not knowing that I should be allowed permission to print this humorous and admirable sketch from the *pen* of our Sir Joshua, I passed over the subject with a slight allusion to the difference between what may be called the two schools of tragic acting. I shall be forgiven, I trust, if I now enter rather farther into it, by printing a few of the most stri From Diderot's Observations on a pamphlet, entitled "Garrick," a critique on the theatres of London and Paris.

king passages of Diderot's tract, as corroborative of Johnson's supposed asser-

tion, which probably contains his true opinion.

"Nature must give the exterior qualities, figure, voice, feeling, judgment, delicacy; but study of great masters, the practice of the stage, labour and reflection, must perfect these gifts of nature. A player formed by imitation may do tolerably; there will be nothing to praise or blame in his playing; but the actor by nature, the actor of genius, is sometimes detestable, sometimes excellent. With whatever severity a novice may be judged, he will have at last the success he merits; hisses silence none but the unqualified.

"And how can nature without art, form a great actor, since nothing passes on the stage exactly as it does in real life, and dramas are composed by convention and on principles?
»

"I would have an actor have a great deal of judgment; I would have him a cool and tranquil spectator of human nature: he must, by consequence, have much delicacy, but no sensibility; or, which is the same thing, the art of imitating every thing, and an equal aptitude to all sorts of characters and parts: if he had sensibility, it would be impossible for him to play ten nights in succession, the same part with the same warmth and success; very warm in the first representation, he would be exhausted and cold as marble at the third: whereas, a reflecting imitator of nature, the first time he appears, he will be the imitator of himself; at the tenth time, far from growing weaker, his play will strengthen itself by all the new reflections he will have made, and you will be moije and more satisfied with him.

"What confirms me in my opinion is the inequality of actors who play from the heart;—never expect any consistency from them; their play is alternately strong and weak, warm and cold, flat and sublime; they will fail to-morrow where they excelled to-day; and they will excel to-morrow, where they failed to-day: whereas those who play by reflection, by study of human nature, by imitation, by memory, are one and the same at all times, equally perfect; all is

understood, all is learnt; their warmth has its beginning, its middle, its end. There are the same accents, the same positions, the same movements; if there is any difference, it is always in favour of the last representation: they are perfect mirrors, always ready to reflect objects, and to exhibit them with the same precision and verity. As well as the poet, they are perpetually drawing from the inexhaustible source of nature, instead of letting be seen directly the extent of their possessions.
«

"And why should the actor differ in this from the statuary, the painter, the orator, the musician? It is not in the paroxysm of the first attempts, that characteristic traits present themselves; they come in tranquil and cool moments, in moments quite unexpected: thus they compare human nature with their own sketch; and the beauties they diffuse over their works, are much more sure of success than those of the first conception. It is not the violent man, the man out of himself, who captivates us; it is the man of self-possession.

"The hot, violent, sensitive men make part of the scene; they afford a spectacle, but they do not represent it. But sensibility is a quality so estimable, that it will not be owned that one can, or that one ought to get rid of it to excel in a profession.—'How?' I shall be asked: Is it not *grief that* produces those plaintive accents from that mother? Is it not actual *sentiment* that inspires it?' By no means: and the proof of this is, that they are measured, that they are part of a system of declamation, that they are subjected to a law of unity, that they concur in the solution of a problem given, that they do not fulfil all the conditions proposed, till after long studies, that in order to execute them exactly, they have been repeated a hundred times: it is because the actor has listened to himself, it is because he hears himself still at the moment in which he disturbs *you,* and that his talent consists not in giving way to his sensibility, as you suppose, but in imitating so perfectly all the exterior signs of sentiment, that you deceive yourself. The cries of grief are noted down in his memory; the attitudes of his despair have been prepared; he knows the precise moment when his tears are to flow: all, all is pure imitation, a lesson learnt before hand, sublime apery, the consciousness of which the actor feels at the moment of executing it, and the memory of which he retains long after he has performed it, but which does not touch his soul, and requires as well as other exercises, only corporal strength. The sock and buskin laid aside, his voice is gone, he feels an extreme fatigue, and gets to bed; but there remains in him neither sorrow nor trouble, nor weakness of mind; 'tis *you*, the audience, who carry away all the impressions.

"The actor is tired, and you are sad; he has made a bustle without feeling any thing, and you have felt without a bustle: were it otherwise, the condition of an actor would be one of the most wretched.

"But happily for us and for him, he *is* not the person; he only plays it.

"I insist then, that it is sensibility which makes the multitude of middling actors, and it is the absence of sensibility which makes sublime actors."

What Horace, Cicero, or Quintilian would have said to this doctrine, is matter of vain curiosity. The often quoted "Si vis me flere, dolendum est Primum ipsi tibi," is supported in the Delphin Horace by the "Ardeat qui vult incendere f" of Cicero, and the "Prius afficiamur ipsi ut alios afficiamus." J And we have talked much, and heard much of the exquisite feelings of those two planets of our stage, Mrs. Siddons and Miss O'Neil. To themselves alone their plan of acquiring feelings, or using those natural to them, can be known, and yet it is probable that even themselves may be unable to trace their own excellence to its source. Any subsequent suffering, Diderot would resolve into the want of " corporal strength."

Certainly, the school of Kemble was a school of evident study, and if we have ever discovered a variation, it may be ascribed to a doubt of the If you wish me to weep, you must first weep yourself.

t Let him burn who would inflame. *t* We must first be affected, that we may affect others. superiority of one mode to another, and the disposition to make the experiment. With Garrick there can be no question: he made known his utter independence on his own feelings; and in his natural manners there certainly was no trace of that sensibility which might be adopted in his great tragic characters. He never, at least in *my* recollection of him, approached nearer to seriousness than being warm to a degree, that to my misapprehension, appeared little short of taking offence; and I was astonished when my father laughed, in reply to what he uttered in these tones.

Amongst our present tragic actors, he whose merits are most the subject of argument, assuredly does not play with that rigid sameness which Diderot considers as the line of improvement; and it is as certain that he is extremely unequal. I was witness to his giving a most extraordinary utterance to those words of indignant complaint in which Richard " descants on" his "own deformity," when the pOet makes him so execrate his form, as to say that the very *dogs* bark at him: he delivered the idea with a vacant look, with the fore-finger of his left hand raised to the side of his nose, and a pause, indicative of the act of listening: I should not have been more surprised had I heard a little yelper at his heels make good his undertaking. I know not whether it be satisfactory, that this is but one of his many manners of playing this arduous character. I am sure it is not one of the best..

A question may be raised, whether the power of exciting strong emotions be the perfection of scenic representation: if it be, the Children in the Wood, be they ever so still, are the best of all possible actors. I saw Mrs. Siddons play Jane Shore, with no feeling but admiration. The story of the play was not new to me; I went to see how *she* would personate the grief and distress which repetition had made familiar to my mind. I saw the same character played very shortly after, at a provincial theatre, by a poor little soul, who could not pro-

nounce an *h* where it was needed, or avoid pronouncing it where it was *not,* and I cried myself half blind; but I could not question which was the better Jane Shore. I should have said that our own actress was above all such weak sacrifices of our feelings — but when I saw her in Mrs. Haller, and this high matron appeared as degraded, without the grand temptation of a monarch's love, I sunk under the oppression, and was not myself for three days. Physicians forbade patients to see her in Isabella, but sent them to see Mrs. Jordan in Little Pickle. Such acting will not soon be forgotten.

I have been, times without number, weary of hearing the pretensions of modern actors compared with those of a former generation. It is a question in which nothing can be proved, because not even effects can be admitted as evidence, unless we could ascertain the judgment of a deceased audience. The claim to praise would be cautiously admitted by persons who may themselves have learned to declaim, and with a near approach to theatrical excellence, the very passages that have obtained applause from the less informed, perhaps by vicious enunciation; therefore, of necessity, as knowledge increases, superiority of excellence is harder to attain, as it becomes harder to say new witty things in proportion as wit is diffused.

I remember old Lady Lucy Meyrick's being prevailed on, perhaps with not less of reluctance than George the Third and his Queen, to see a tragedy, for the sake of seeing Mrs. Siddons. We were curious to learn what impression had been made on her mind by that which so forcibly impressed that of the public. She acknowledged the execution of the character very fine, yet not to be compared with what she remembered of former actors. "In short," she concluded, "I must say, that compared with Mrs. Pritchard and Mrs. Cibber, Mrs. Siddons's grief is the grief of a cheesemonger's wife." This was easily to be understood; the time of quick impression was gone, but the remembrance of it remained. I presume it could not be in Lady Macbeth that Mrs. Siddons had been so judged; and I should suppose the idea wore out, for if I am correct in my memory, her ladyship followed Mrs. Siddons as completely through her characters, and even in repetitions of them, as she could have followed the favourites of her younger days. It was, however, impossible to withhold credit from one point of praise, in which she considered Mrs. Cibber as unrivalled; this was in singing "God save the King" in chorus on the stage, — she said it was a perfect hymn as *she* sang it; and indeed so it ought always to be, and so we trust it is felt by him for whom with such true British loyalty it is offered up. What do we not owe to those counsels and those counsellors, who, by saving us from anarchy and confusion, have preserved to such as *have* feelings, those perhaps the highest of the human mind, and made still higher by Our dear and venerable friend, Colonel H, did more for me as a child than he perhaps could recollect. I remember, long before he had attained a middle age, that his conversation, without departing from the most agreeable cheerfulness, contained those results of thought to which a life of campaigning is seldom conducive. Some one remarking at my father's table on the infrequency of seeing very elderly persons at a tragedy, he shook his head, and said, "They have probably seen too much of tragedy in reality." Another of his preceptive remarks has contributed very much to my domestic quiet. A wine-glass being broken,' he observed on the unfairness of severity on such accidents, if we consider how much more servants have to do with these brittle possessions than we ourselves have. Hearing this before I had any power to transgress, it was in time to guide my practice, and I probably owe to it the repose of my conscience, and the retaining many a good servant.

being blended, the united feelings of piety, loyalty, and love for our country!

I have said, heretofore, in speaking of Garrick, that my father more frequently admired him in comedy than in tragedy. I might have added, that in love-scenes, Barry was considered as rivalling him. This I can easily conceive, and I should

question whether these were not the parts least agreeable to Garrick. To have recalled to his mind the time of his early passion, and I never heard of more than one, would have been, I sup Is the reply of Quin to a slip-slop milliner at Bath very trite? I never heard it but from Sir J. H. This caricaturist of sensibility was detaining Quin, while buying a pair of gloves, with expressions of her ardent desire to see him make love. Quin, who seems to have been the Dr. Johnson of the stage, if we may judge from the character of his replies, answered, "Madam, I never *make* love; I always buy it *ready made."*

But he once met with his match when visiting Lord Holmes, in that abode of rural wit, the Isle of Wight. Quin had lost his dog; meeting a poor man, he told him of his loss, concluding with, " I hope you are honest here." "Yes," replied the man, "I believe so; but there is a stranger down at my Lord's, and mayhap he may know of your dog." pose, to have forfeited his friendship for ever. He was a great instance of that entire change of conduct which so many plead as impossible; he quitted a mode of life in itself erroneous, to practise that which was in every way most exemplary.— Return we to our deserted philosopher.

That Johnson treated without mercy all false pretensions is true, and certainly worthy of imitation, and the fear of seeming to make them, kept, perhaps, more persons than myself from him. In my own instance, I cannot repent that I felt it. The instinctive sensation has preserved me in a state the most conducive to happiness. Those who choose to sit on the ground are not easily dismounted; and those who concur with Johnson in thinking themselves morally the least meritorious of all their acquaintance, are not likely to squabble for laurels in literature.

I perfectly remember, on one of those days when I was not in high favour, my father's saying, "Miss," which was my designation of disgrace, "I intend to take you to Dr. Johnson's this evening." It came to my ear in the same form as a threat some years before, when we were

all three *under a cloud* for some exertion of *fidelity* in what Sir J. used to call, at such times, "the triple alliance:" — the threat was that we should all be taken to see King Lear!! It would have amused a by-stander, to witness the ferment this denunciation of vengeance occasioned: my elder brother probably would have acquiesced, and by prudence disappointed the purpose; the younger would possibly have turned restive, and stood in immovable resolution; as to myself, I made a friend of my mother, and represented that if I was incapacitated from labour, by the effect on my nerves, nothing would be got. The offence was, perhaps, little more than some sullenness I had shown, on being called back from a projected walk round the Park to copy for the printer, and my brothers' refusing to condemn me. Bad enough on *my* part, I confess, for it was disobedience; but my labour was hard, and my pleasures were few — so I forgive myself.

From the visit to Dr. Johnson, I could not, however, get off: but here I behaved worse; for I revenged myself by the wretched expedient of listening and replying, exclusively, to the inanities of one of his inmates, Mrs. Desmoulins. I am sure Johnson neither saw me nor heard me; but I stayed my time out, and as there was nothing said "in the bond" about being agreeable, or making up to the Doctor, I was acquitted. Even my father had nothing to say; for I was *en regie.*

It may be said of Johnson, that he had a peculiar individual feeling of regard towards his many and various friends, and that he was to each what I might call the indenture, or counterpart of what they were to him. My brother says, that any memoirs of his conversations with Lord Thurlow or Burke would be invaluable: to the former he acknowledged that he always "talked his best;" and the latter would, by the force of his own powers, have taxed those of Johnson to the utmost. But still the inquisitive world, that world whose inquisitiveness has tempted almost to sacrilege, would not have been satisfied without the minor communications of

Boswell, though he sometimes sorely punctured his friend to get at what he wanted.

It has always appeared wonderful to me, that even under the strong impulse of such curiosity, what Miss Seward had to tell, and she certainly had much to tell, was not received with more avidity. Whether it was, that just at the time of publishing her Correspondence, which is as entertaining in matter and manner as Mr. Boswell's Memoirs, the world did not wish to see their favourite represented so without adumbration, in the colours that did not flatter him, or that they were justly indignant at the revelations concerning not only others but herself, of this enamoured modern Sappho, I never could divine; but certainly poor Miss Seward, had she lived, would not have been made vainer than she was, by the reception of her volumes; perhaps I may be told it was unnecessary, or, perhaps, that it would have been a vain attempt to render her so — *mats cela n'est pas mon affaire.* We all blamed her, nay, we all condemned her j but we read and confessed her very entertaining.

If I were called on to name the person with whom Johnson might have been seen to the fairest advantage, *I* should certainly name Mr. Langton; not that I consider his mind as a forcing-pump to Johnson's; but because it would have left the latter to its freedom of action, by gently exercising it, and that in the best way. Mr. Langton's good-breeding, and the pleasing tone of his voice, would have given the pitch to Johnson's replies; his classic acquirements would have brought out those of the other speaker; while the thorough respect Johnson entertained for him, would have prevented that harshness which sometimes alarmed a third person. And in Mr. Langton's family, as a visitor, Johnson must have found employment for all the tenderness of his feelings, without any counteracting irritation. Lady Rothes was not by birth Scotch,— this was in her favour; and the tones of that country, which she had acquired by early transplantation and long residence, were such as, from *her,* could of-

fend no one's ear. She was eminently handsome, and had a person dignified without heaviness, or exceeding the common proportions; her manners were the most easy; and though entertaining and showing a higher respect for all distinctions than could be demanded from her, nothing could embarrass or make her appear otherwise than perfectly at home. Her sweet complacent smile was a welcome wherever it met a friend; and the remarkable modesty of her look and demeanour, might have made her a fit *sitter* for a Madonna: her features expressed thought and good sense, and her sincerity gave value to every profession she made. I remember perfectly that when under family sorrow, in which she had felt neglected by an intimate friend, she unexpectedly received a letter of hackneyed apology and fulsome fondness, from the lady, she said to me, with a very just sense of the feeble attempt, that she would reply to the letter by a visit, and not by writing, as she could thus avoid even the deviation from sincerity which the subscription of her name would demand.

Of the children of the family, Dr. Johnson was very fond — they were, in their full number, ten, with not a plain face, nor a faulty person. Alas, now how reduced! They were taught to behave to Johnson as they would have done to a grandfather; and he felt it. Lady Rothes was always obliging, and at the table of Mr. Langton he met Paoli, General Oglethorpe, and many others, most of whom I have already named, who excited his spirits very agreeably.

Mr. Langton's situation in Lincolnshire, at a place bearing his own name, was not lost on Johnson: he could indeed extract satisfaction in contemplating the affluence resulting from what are called "great concerns;" but the rank of an English gentleman, with good ancestry, an affluent income, and the possibility of rising to any height which is afforded by talent, must have been, in his judgment, as it was in that of our venerable George the Third, one of the most to be desired and respected.

The contemplative turn of mind, and lowly Christianity of Mr. Langton, must

have admirably harmonised with the tendency of Johnson's; and this it was that made him utter the wish that " his spirit might be with that of Langton." Neither La Trappe nor the Grand Chartreux could have sent out a disciple more awfully impressed with those feelings which almost overwhelmed Johnson, than Bennet Langton; and that these feelings were attended with some inconvenient want of activity was not always perceptible, where a wife was at hand to order or to do. Mr. Langton's great height, six feet six inches, might be some cause of this inertness, but more was ascribable to the constitution of his mind. He fulfilled the injunction of the pious Sir Thomas Browne, to "sit quietly in the soft showers of Providence."

But on one occasion, I remember Johnson's departing from his gentleness towards Mr. Langton, and in his irritation showing some inconsistency of ideas. I went with my father to call in Bolt Court, one Sunday after church. There were many persons in the Doctor's drawing-room, and among them Mr. Langton, who stood leaning against the post of an open door, undergoing what I suppose the giver of it would have called an "objurgation." Johnson, on my father's entrance, went back to explain the cause of this, which was no less than that Mr. Langton, in his opinion, ought then to have been far on his road into Lincolnshire, where he was informed his mother was very ill. Mr. Langton's pious affection for his mother could not be doubted, — she was a parent of whom any son might have been proud; but this was a feeling which never could have been brought into the question by her son: the inert spirit, backed, perhaps, by hope, and previous knowledge of the extent of similar attacks, prevailed; and Johnson's arguments seemed hitherto rather to have rivetted Mr. Langton's feet to the place where he was, than to have spurred him to quit it. My father, thus referred to, took up the subject, and a few half-whispered sentences from him made Mr. Langton take his leave: but, as he was quitting the room, Johnson with one of his howls, and his indescribable but really pathetic slow semi-circuits of his head, said most energetically, "Do, Hawkins, teach Langton a little of the world."

How the usage of the world could be made applicable to such a case, I confess I do not see, nor did I ever on any other occasion hear of Johnson's conforming himself to this usage. That he thought himself polite or well-bred we have his own testimony; and in the Sunday-visit to which I allude, I had indeed an opportunity of observing him, when making an effort to be complimentary. He was, at the time, fast declining, and Mrs. Reynolds, the sister of Sir Joshua, sent to make enquiries. His answer was, "Tell her I can *not* be well, for she does *not* come to see me." And verily he looked round on those in the room, as if he expected applause for this hyperbolical effusion towards' one who, as far as I could ever judge, possessed nothing sufficiently characteristic to call for it; unless, indeed, he were paying her " in her own coin," for the indiscriminate adulation and courtly acquiescence of *her* civility. I cannot describe my own feeling of surprise, and I was going to say contempt.

Brought up, as my brothers and myself were, in a strict regard to truth, and in abhorrence of all insincerity, even that of fashion, we often stared when other children would have been pleased, and saw as clearly through unmerited eulogiums bestowed on ourselves as on others. The habit of truth grew up, and sometimes made us too exacting. It rendered me once very sharp-sighted to the embarrassment of a dignitary of the church, of the first order of elegance, and who was patronised by the Bentinck family. In one of the Dean's visits, my father was speaking of the then Dowager Duchess of Portland, distinguished at that time not more for her birth, than for her fine taste and rich vein of conversation. The Dean acquiesced in all this, but in terms so general, as to make my father appear the better informed eulogist, which he could not be, as I do not recollect his ever having been in company with her Grace, or to have seen her

nearer, perhaps, than at St. James's. At last, some question or observation betrayed to the parties that they were unconsciously speaking

Johnson's associations and elections of acquaintances were reducible to no rule. Need on the one hand, and the power to help on the other, did certainly render him most charitably blind to all delinquency, and deaf to all the dictates of caution and prudence. Whether that unquestioning facility be in itself good, which, if imitated to any extent, would, as far as it reached, do mischief, requires consideration; but I can feelingly assert that, after his death, the demerits of many of those whom he sheltered, became conspicuous.

Mrs. Anna Williams I remember as long as I can remember any one. While residing in Johnson's house, her only home, she gave a sort of creditable consistency to the *menage,* and, being herself a gentlewoman, conferred on her protector the character of gentleman. Together with him, before he was ingulfed at Streatham, she often, in the course of the winter, dined with my father and mother, and frequently without other company. I see her now, a pale shrunken old lady, dressed in scarlet made in the handsome French fashion of the time, with a lace cap, with two stiffened projecting wings on the temples, and a black lace hood over it; her grey or powdered hah" appearing. Her temper has been recorded as marked with the Welsh fire, and this might be excited by some of the meaner inmates of the upper floors; but her gentle kindness to *me* I never shall forget, or think consistent with a *bad* temper. I well recollect, on hearing of the levity of two young women in our neighbourhood on the death of their mother, her describing, with the tenderest feeling, the better conduct of a young friend of hers; and I know nobody from whose discourse there was a greater chance of deriving high ideas of moral rectitude. Her making tea without the help of sight, and doing various other things which' required it, were talked of *then* as wonderful. I have heard it, indeed, hinted, that her mode of ascertaining the fulness of the

cups, was little short of what, in a trial of *dry* heat, is called actual cautery; but as I love her memory, I hope she made her appeal to the outside of the cup.

of different personages. My father meant the *dowager,* the Dean was thinking on the *reigning* Duchess, too much had been said to get round neatly; therefore confessing his error, he repeated, "Both very charming — both of fine taste, both full of anecdote, very clever women indeed." Now as one of these ladies was certainly as much beyond seventy, as the other was beyond thirty; as the dowager was the sole daughter of the second earl of Oxford, had been the theme of poets, and was the enviable possessor of" The Vase," and of a collection unrivalled by that of any lover of *virtu;* as years and situations had filled her mind with ideas, and stored her memory with anecdotes, I could by no means digest this palliation of a misunderstanding, or consider as within the rule of straight-forward proceeding, this oblique mode of what has been latterly denominated "*backing-out."*

The immortalised Frank, the *faithful* black servant of Dr. Johnson, could scarcely, I think, less deserve the reflected credit given him. What he would have done by or with his master in case of extremity, I do not wish to surmise, but I know certainly that he took bribes for denying him to others, when Mr. Steevens wanted his assistance in his Shakspeare, and, I believe, it is incontestable that, *vice versa,* he sold intelligence to Boswell.

When my father had to carry the will into effect, he was obstructed in every way by Francis. As fast as he drew money, so fast he spent it, and came for more. I remember seeing him, with all the vulgar insolence of a hackneycoachman, chuck up a few halfpence, which, he said, without rendering any reason, were all he had remaining of a large sum which he had received very shortly before, and urging Sir J. H. most indecorously to precipitation for which he might have been called to account; and this, when, had it not been that my father laboured the point incessantly, Francis, after all his master's vain boasting, and unfeeling disregard of nearer connections, would have been left to the labour of his hands for a subsistence. My father then lost all consideration for the fellow, who, as if he had had only the justification of the acting executor in view, as quickly as possible reduced himself to the refuge of a workhouse.

When the funeral was to be arranged, and a proper person to conduct it, was to be treated with, Francis interposed a low connection of his wife's, and Sir J. H. very wisely gave way, considering, perhaps, that he who had lived like Johnson, needed not to be buried with the precision of rank; the numerous attendance of friends spoke sufficiently that it was no common personage whose remains were conveying to the mausoleum of royalty, learning, genius, and wit.

Few persons know what my father went through in performing these last acts of steady unobtrusive friendship. They were called for in the depth of one of the two severest winters that ever I remember, immediately following each other, and with little intervention of summer; the snow had fallen in October, and an unrelenting frost intruded so far into the spring, that on the first of May, not a leaf had opened on the trees in St. James's Park; on the fifth they were in foliage! Again the snow came, if I recollect right, in October, and in December, when Johnson died, none but hackney-horses could be risked in the streets. My father disregarded every thing; he was little at home in the day, and if he returned at midnight, only giving fresh orders for the morning, we were happy.

To conclude this period, and resume the idea of Sir J. H. as Johnson's biographer, I will tell what I recollect or know to be fact. I think it was immediately on his emancipation from this severe attendance, that I heard my father say, speaking of the recent demise," He has left me his executor, and I will write his life. " His admiration of Johnson then stood very high. A very few hours after, perhaps not more than four, two gentlemen came to him. Wanting me to write, he ordered me to be called into his study, and on my entering the room, he named these visitors to me as Mr. Strahan and Mr. Cadell. Tne next movement was my father's I will not interrupt the text with a trifling anecdote, but as a singular coincidence, the reader may be amused with knowing into what a situation I had inadvertently drawn myself. Some few years previous to this time, being in want of a sum of money for a whim of girlish patronage, and having no *honest* means of raising it, I wrote a downright novel. It could do nobody any harm— indeed *I* thought it a marvellous moral performance, as it punished the culprits and rewarded the virtuous of my *dramatis personce* —but it was a temerarious undertaking, as descriptive of manners and situations of which I knew little but by hearsay. It was done in the secrecy of a coiner, my only confidential friend being my younger brother. Not at all foreseeing the open contact into which I might be called with any bookseller, I had written to Cadell on the subject of publishing my manuscript—he had declined it, unless he might know the writer. I was not ignorant of the sagacious scent of these agents between authors and the public; and when called on to write what Mr. Cadell was to see, I dreaded his recognition of my handwriting, and his incautiously betraying me; but the matter, I suppose, had slipped out of his mind, and I escaped harmless. 'On this subject, may I be allowed to say a few words more? The manuscript was published for me by Hookham, who, as I have elsewhere stated, was content to remain in ignorance, and who most honourably sent me for it, twice as much as I needed, and most kindly encouraged me to proceed. I had coming into our sitting-room, and observing on the singularity of his being requested to do that had the good fortune to please the then taste of the reader of such works; and amongst others, a lady, now living in the neighbourhood of Windsor, and whose good opinion was very valuable, favoured the work by an ardent curiosity to trace it to the writer, but Hookham could not satisfy her; and though I wrote many subsequent volumes, I still preserved my *incognito.* I scarcely know why I acted thus clandestinely. I wag certainly afraid of some displeasure, and I was ashamed of my employment; and though my father sometimes urged me to write, and wished to have introduced me into a literary correspondence, I preferred my obscurity, though it forced me to exertions of industry, which nothing but the *con amorc* of application could have enabled me to make, when I had no time but what I could *purloin,* and was writing six hours in the day for my father, and reading aloud to my mother nearly as long. But two thousand pages never daunted me. I learnt Italian, and extracted from every book that came in my way; I made as large a part of my clothes as could be made at home; I worked muslin; I learnt botany; and I was my mother's storekeeper. Air and exercise were little thought on. I aired indeed with Lady H. in the carriage, but I read or worked.

At length, after the death of my father, I revealed myself under the strictest confidence to my kind, generous, worthy publisher, after which I wrote but once; and here occurred the circumstance, perhaps, too circuitously prefaced. This last manuscript lay on Hookham's desk, when this lady one day went into the library. She asked what it was, and was told that it was a work from the pen that had so often excited her enquiries. She naturally repeated them—but Hookham was firm.

Happening to call there again in a short time, she saw a which he had resolved on. He said that the booksellers meant to collect and publish Johnson's works, and had spontaneously commissioned Mr. Strahan and Mr. Cadell to ask him to write the life that was to preface them, and to oversee the whole publication. Considering the necessary expenses of such an undertaking, they had offered him 200/. which allowed him to employ an amanuensis, and to turn over the correction of the press to others. He added a question, however, whether / would undertake the labour, saying, "It will be a large octavo volume of 600 or 700 pages: it is a trifling job to *you,* and as for that part of the corrections with which I shall concern myself, you are so used to it, that it will be nothing."

I think at that time a new edition of the Complete Angler found me employment; but I would have undertaken any thing even without pay, for the various knowledge I gained. My father was no ungenerous exactor: he had often repeated to us the axiom, that no one had a right to the gratuitous service of another; and the caveat of the Jewish law against muzzling the ox while treading out the corn, was so constantly in his mind, that he never suffered me even to peel an orange for him, without giving me what, as children, we called "two pigs." He, therefore, in this spirit, offered me at the time such a remuneration as I joyfully accepted, and eventually trebled it—I had forty pounds!

drawing which I had sent to him to get framed, and with it a note, which lay open on the desk. Mrs. asked whose property the drawing was, and as there was here no cause for concealment, he told her, and turned the note towards her. The note was, I dare say, written in a much fairer hand than my copy for the printer, but Mrs. immediately said, "The writer of that note, is the writer of these anonymous works." To the lady's honour, and that of our sex, I must add, that for fear of doing me harm, not only this lady, but one who accompanied her, inviolably kept my secret. *Of* the life, as my father wrote it, I have no occasion to speak, and *for* it, even *he* would not expect me to say any thing. We, to our shame be it spoken! were most unmerciful critics; he gave up every thing—'tis too little to say to our *judgment,* though his expression often was, as he threw Is there no work existing, or no deeply read scholar disposed to write one, that shall elucidate the wisdom, the mercy, and the fine contrivance of the Mosaic institutions? The specimen above quoted, is sufficient to excite a suspicion that we possess in the Pentateuch treasures of recondite beneficence, that need only good-will and thought to bring them to light. his rough draught amongst us, " What you would have it make it;"—it was given up to *am feroci-*

ty: the *facon* of our hard work was often merriment, and his good-humour admitted of our receiving the flying leaves, with "Come, let us see;" and when we objected, we condescended to say "We would see what we could make of it."

In *general,* I must say, my father's disposition to give up while thus employed was incredible. With the History of Music, we dared not take liberties; and there were times in the course even of this *minor* undertaking, when the best judgment amongst us could not prevail.

A report got abroad, from my father's showing Mr. Langton some assistance which I had given, that I had written the Life; but I furnished no more than the reviews of the works connected with the subject.

In reviewing the Scotch Tour, I had contrasted, in rather handsome terms, the prejudices of Johnson with the candid good-humour of Pennant; and for this, Sir J. received the very polite thanks of the latter, in a bookseller's shop. He could not avow the fact — his revision of what I had done acquitted him of any thing unfair, and he very honourably brought the acknowledgments to me.

To speak of the volumes which my father was to publish. I confess I had great expectation of seeing in them the " Marmor Norfolciense." The time was passed, I thought, when any thing written against the Protestant succession could be offensive, and we were at a point of time when such an obstinate adherence was rising in estimation. The departure from these principles was far more heinous to *my* apprehension; and perhaps I should have liked the publication of the exceptionable production the better for exhibiting this, and allowing me in my father's chatty minutes to run him hard on the subject: but he had much more wisdom than his daughter; and I could always perceive that he very unwillingly communicated any thing on the subject. On the contrary, he would quote, though not at all resembling the case, his own change of political opinion as he gained experience; and having lived to see the necessity of that temperament which tolerates some evil for

the sake of much good, he would advert, with merriment at his own zeal, to a period when with all his heart he could have set fire to a train that should have blown up Sir Robert Walpole.

Of the works which my father had to collect and publish, I can say little worth attention. The Rasselas, cold, stiff, dry, and dejecting, as it is, has been increasing in favour with its age, and is now become the touchstone by which ladies prove their power of translating into Italian. I once said to Mrs. Welch that I liked Hawkesworth's Almoran and Hamet far better. She replied, by bidding me read them again—I did so, and was astonished at my former preference. The moral and religious papers in Johnson's periodical works can be duly valued by those only who have sought consolation under affliction; and it is very remarkable, that they are replete with that comfort and support, which seemed, alas! at one time almost to have failed their author. The lighter parts of these works, particularly such as affect to trifle, and to portray female character, are often and justly blamed as wanting that pliancy of discrimination which is essential in small characteristics. Instead of a glove, he presents a boot.

Of his detached and miscellaneous biographical pieces, or such as are the result of thought, the merit is as various as the subjects; and in reading many of them, it may occur to those familiar with his style, that it is often kept down — and sometimes with difficulty. This is, perhaps, no where more evident than in those sermons, which are published under the name of Dr. Taylor of Westminster; and the restraint seems to have been intolerable, for the secret betrays itself perpetually. At the time these were preached, we lived in Westminster, and our parish-church being that of Dr. Taylor's preferment, we heard them, as did Johnson himself, when he spent his Sunday with the preacher. My father made no scruple of attacking him on the subject — he preserved a profound silence.

Of the many uncouth friendships which Johnson formed, this with Dr.

Taylor would have been one of the most surprising and least creditable; but it had begun in youth and adversity; therefore its continuance was pardonable in a man so privileged as Johnson, and with feelings so under the dominion of a diseased mind; but I have heard of proceedings in the Court of Chancery, which showed his moral character to be so inconsistent with his profession, that it needed almost the tie of consanguinity to justify the continuance of intercourse.

Dr. Taylor was a strange kind of man: I know not whether I ought to call him *eccentric,* as that implies a disposition to fly off, and there was a heaviness about him, that must have made *his* movements tend downwards. In Westminster, where he had a prebend, he lived in a handsome style, kept his chariot, and appeared like a dignitary of the church. He lived on a milk diet, which gave him a very disagreeable complexion; and when one of my brothers has called on him, he has dragged forth and exhibited his will, exultingly pointing out his adoption of the ancient form of, "In the name of the Holy Trinity," &c. A suit which was *pending,* as I am bid to call the process of such a business, in the Court of Chancery, occasioned much mirth to the young lawyers. The question arose from a will by which the testator bequeathed a very considerable property, and Dr. Taylor was to be much benefited. One of the points sworn to in the pleadings, was, that after making the will, some of those who had an interest in it, would follow the testator, who was infirm and heavy, up or down his staircase, the balustrade of which was very crazy, to *assist* him, in a *proper direction,* in case of his swaying towards the *dangerous* side. The *intention* was sworn to; but *we* have nothing to do with *intentions;* nor do I know whether, in such proceedings, deponents are required or expected to be very literal.

The Lives of the Poets was the portion of Johnson's works for which the public had the greatest relish. "Tell us what to think," is the silent re The necessity of using this word, gives me an opportunity of preserving an anecdote

of my father's. Lord Hardwicke, in a time of war, made use in the House of Peers of the term *pendente hello.* Lord Carteret, who was a first-rate scholar, corrected him, by saying, in a high tone, Pendente Wo? my Lord! Flagrante *bello.* quest of so many readers, that the success of them was secure. Readers of a higher class might be pleased in comparing his opinions with their own; and others, able to predict the manner in which Johnson would use this opportunity, were curious to see how far his great powers would carry him. Beside these, there were others whose mental vision would be far better consulted by presenting strong light and shade to it, than by offering those blended colours, which softening into each other, leave to the beholder the labour of developing the method of the artist. These were very sure of wh atthey sought from the pencil of Johnson.

If facts were expected, there was little to gratify; for the work was meant to be slight: and Johnson fulfilled this meaning, by absolutely refusing information with regard to Pope, which my father had taken the opportunity of a summer-breakfast with Lord Mansfield, to get from his Lordship. I conclude that it was Mrs. Welch who suggested the taking for the model of these Has Sir J. H. any where said that Lord Mansfield showed him a portrait of Betterton painted by Pope? He did so.

"Lives," as they were called, the sketches of Madame D'Aunois prefixed to a similar work of the French; but as I am not acquainted with these, I cannot state the degree of resemblance.

But whatever might be the expectation of the public, it was gratified by the agreeable excitation of witnessing or partaking the vacillations of an intellect, that could make the reasons for and against any question, now lighter, now more weighty. Johnson played at see-saw; and in watching him, his admirer could almost fancy himself mounted on the other end of the plank.

It might be entertainment to many: to myself, as I may have hinted, it was the most fatiguing wear and tear of mind, that any writing could inflict. I remem-

ber particularly the criticism on Rowe's plays which tormented me beyond measure. At one moment I coveted them as works of the highest standard, and most virtuous interest; and I resolved on buying them: the next page changed my opinion and lowered my respect; and I rejoiced in having escaped the waste of money. My father's opinion, indeed, rather disposed me to forbearance: he did not entirely condemn them, and he had f great respect for the family of Rowe; but all pathos of what he called the *maudlin* sort, he contemned heartily; and from this characteristic, Rowe is not always exempt.

I had still many waverings, that is to say, just as many as Johnson, before I settled the question with regard to Rowe's tragedies. At length I bought them, and found that, to judge fairly, they must be considered individually. But I could have sold them again at half the cost, when, in one instance particularly, I was forced to rank their author with those moral writers who, under the semblance of purifying the minds of their readers, make their own wade through a sea of corruption.

My father was, I think, much vexed at the introduction of Pomfret, whose productions he called "chambermaids poetry." Had he heard one of us quote a line from any of these his *maudlin* writers, or express any admiration of Hervey's Meditations, I think he would have given us up as incorrigible.

A very kind *mediating* lady of his acquaintance once wished to recommend to him for a wife her niece, afterwards the celebrated Mrs. Barry, the actress: he was not very likely to be drawn in; but if he had wavered, the method taken to secure him would have saved him. The young lady was a visitor in the house at the same time with himself. As a correct young man, it was to be presumed that industry and attention to religion would meet his approbation. Miss S was therefore at work with " The Practice of Piety" by her, and as he was known to be fond of music, she was desired to sing; and she sung as he used to describe it, about " *mutal* love."

Another lady was put forward by her

friends in the year 1745, but unfortunately, the poor girl, in her zeal for the House of Brunswick, talked of the *veterian* corps, and he broke the meshes.

On the appearance of these Lives of the Poets, as they were called, I looked anxiously for that of Young, as one on which his favourite labour might be best employed. My father's opinion of the Night Thoughts was the least settled of any that I ever sought from him. When I had asked him to direct my judgment, he replied, "I really hardly know what to say; and as I cannot decide for myself, I cannot fairly do it for you. The Narcissa has been commended by able men, and there are parts of it very fine; but the whole is a favourite with the vulgar, and you know that is not a recommendation with me. I remember on their first appearance they were thought the production of ' mad Tom Hervey,' rather than of Young, who was himself a timeserving, obsequious i parson, not at all the man of his own poetry; but read for yourself, and you will judge."

But Young, as a man and a poet, has long found his "due level. His wild incoherence cannot depreciate the great truths which he so solemnly urges. The subject of everlasting happiness or misery, cannot be materially injured by a little occasional bad taste, or egotising obtrusion; and it would have been important satisfaction to see Johnson weigh his beauties against his defects: but into this field for criticism he had suffered another to intrude, and we had more facts indeed, but less of what was desirable, from the far inferior pen of Herbert Croft. Lord Palmerston, in consequence of Young's connection by marriage with his family, was very solicitous to get some errors corrected in the re-publication of the poet's The place of Young's residence was visited, a short time after his death, by a friend of my father's, who was curious to see the scenery in which he had framed his mind. It bore no analogy to his cast of thought; and from a servant who had lived with him, he learned that no two things could have less of affinity than Young's habits of life, and his meditations on the most important points in

human existence. His gravity was hardly enough for a-gownsman of any description.

Life. This concern, I know, brought his Lordship frequently to our house; and I believe he took on himself to make the alterations he wished for. *Loquitur H. H.)*

"Johnson had many years before, written, in a far more elaborate manner, the life of his early friend, Savage; it was, consequently, a great saving of labour to print nearly *verbatim,* as the life of the poet, what he had written as that of a friend. The bulkiness, therefore, of this one life, must not be taken as any proof of the comparative importance of Savage's writings, which certainly are not of any superior merit, nor are they indicative of that genius which the world often accepts as an apology for great irregularity of moral conduct.

"Johnson's opinion of Gray is well known; and many persons attacked him for what he had written concerning him. I remember to have heard him say, 'Why can they not let me have my opinions?' alleging as a reason for their so doing, that false criticism is its own punishment. Perhaps it may be too much to say, that he is always right, or always wrong; neither his praise nor his censure can always be relied on, and his commendation of those stanzas in the Elegy written in a Country Churchyard, beginning with, 'Yet even these stones,' is as much to be attributed to the morbid melancholy of his own mind, as to any canons of criticism to be learned either from Longinus or Quintilian.

"Where the question'of religion or piety did not intervene, as in the instance of Addison, the circumstance of Whig or Tory, Oxford or Cambridge, had no small influence in the forming of his opinions; and in many points, not connected with such subjects, Johnson's mind was far from settled, and *that* even at a time of life when most men, almost from necessity, seek refuge from doubt, in laying down certain maxims of wisdom or prudence, from which it would be inexpedient or morally wrong to deviate."

The Irene, that fine closet-drama, was printed with the poetry of Johnson. Compared with *plays* it is lost. I heard Steevens, in one of his declamatory fits, discuss and quote its excellencies, and say, ""If it had not been for the strangling Irene on the stage, it would have succeeded, but *that* the audience would not bear."

The business of editing Johnson's Works brought to our house many literary persons, in some way or other interested in the undertaking. Amongst others, Richard Paul Joddrell, with whom my father was previously acquainted, and who was one of the elegant and classical *literati* of the time. He came with rather more of ceremony than was absolutely necessary, even when gentlemen considered external appearances as indicative of rank; and the business of his first call was to communicate a translation which he had made of Johnson's two lines on the lady familiarly called Molly Aston, but who was of a baronet's family. She was a wit and a whig, and, as my father has styled her, " a declaimer for liberty." Johnson's lines were, — I wonder what Steevens would have thought had he lived to witness the present state of public taste; when, if we may judge by that in other things, the cry of " more murders," "more Irenes," "more stranglings," seems the more probable demand. We are advancing fast in that circuit of opinion which leads back to raw-head and bloody-bones, hobgoblins »nd witches.

"Liber ut esse velim, suasisti, pulchra Maria,

Ut maneam liber — pulchra Maria vale!"

Mr. Joddrell rendered them, —

"When fair Maria's soft persuasive strain

Bids universal liberty to reign,

Oh! how at variance are her lips and eyes!

For while the charmer talks, the gazer dies."

Now I must confess, that by altering the first line, so as to make it end with *"persuasion tries,"* the second and fourth might have been withdrawn, which would have left the translation somewhat more like the original than it is at present. But this composition did not come to us to be criticised; the author, I believe, came to see that it was properly inserted, and correct, and then, probably, to return acknowledgments.

My brother Harry, at the first mention of this translation, was curious to see how a scholar, and an elegant scholar, a character of which he was himself emulous, wrote poetry. He knew that some busde had been made on the subject of Molly Aston, and that the translator had spoken of the great difficulty of compressing the sense, in which point he had certainly failed. Instantly on casting his eye on the lines, and without referring to the original, he said, "Why not thus?—

"In vain, dear girl, thou bidst me to be free:
I lose my freedom when I look on thee.
"

Had he considered, he might have gone still closer, by making the last line, —

"Freedom to gain — Mary, adieu to thee!"

My father very reluctantly adopted Mr. Joddrell's, — there was no choice; and so ended this vehement sensation.

The publication of the Latin poems called for a council, in which some were for suppressing them as of doubtful Latinity; some were for lenity to such errors, in consideration of *sentiment;* and some, like those spectators of theatrical representations who are determined to have the full value for their money, insisted on having every thing. His Sapphic Ode to Mrs. Thrale is admirable, and rendered doubly valuable by Miss Knight's exquisite translation; and his religious effusions, in whatever language written, show the important use which he, sick in body and mind as he often was, made of moments that might have been profitable only in learning to suffer. That line in his Vanity of Human Wishes, in which he allows, as one subject of prayer that may safely be offered up to the Throne of Grace, —

"patience, sovereign o'er transmuted ill," is in itself a text.

It is to be regretted that the pursuits of intellect, as well as the various species of manual operations, carry their concomitant ill with them. To the irritability of an author, there was added, in Johnson's frame, that of a martyr to an incurable disease; an irritability which was still further increased by the toughness of his spirit, which made all his sufferings the imprisoned companions of his own bosom. "I hate a complainer," was one of his strong expressions condemning a weakness of which he certainly was not guilty. Under the conviction of his endurances, his friends might be more assiduous to please and amuse him; but he was not to be *coaxed,* nor was the state of his mind or feelings sufficiently steady to enable even those who loved and honoured him the most, to perfect their good wishes. I will not, by disturbing the text, *compel* the reader to peruse a little narrative, which I yet wish to bring forward, as explanatory of some circumstances connected with the life, the character, and posthumous reputation of a true descendant of the *irritabile genia,* who left behind him for publication, a work by which he obtained money from a bookseller, but which he could not have dared to produce to the light himself. *Hit talents* were never sufficient to palliate *his* waywardness; he was a clergyman, excusing himself from the duties of his profession, on the plea of his irritability of nerves; and he made a living by writing for authors who could not rely on their own abilities. Too much cannot be said in praise of his industrious endeavours to support a family of several children. He had most of the requisites for being agreeable, if not valuable; but they were all ruined by his unbounded use of the privilege of his class in the indulgence of a capricious temper.

With this labourer in the fields of literature, I had been acquainted in the common routine of London intimacy, and probably should have lessened even this, on the occurrence of some circumstances not creditable to his judgment, had not a sudden reverse of fortune, or rather a second failure in prudence, excited my compassion for him, and occasioned me great anxiety for his amiable

and exemplary wife, a woman, to whose charms of person, manners, and conversation, he had been much indebted for the tenacity of some of his best friends. I hastened to them on the news of the disaster, and, to take away all fear that this severe blow should alienate my

We must nevertheless admire and revere that honest disposition to abide the worst, and to family from them, I pressed him and Mrs. to make us a week's visit.

A day was fixed; I fetched our guests, and certainly had a specimen of his preference of parental regards to the duties of good manners, by his inviting one of his sons, at parting from him, to come and share the visit, and when *he* did not come, to send a brother in his stead. A footboy also was ordered to bring letters daily, and "to take his dinner" on his arrival. This could hardly be done without some apology, but it was turned into a compliment, in his accounting for the liberty he took, by his knowing it was " the style" of our house. How he had discovered this *style,* I know not, but by the inspiration of the moment; it is, however, in truth," a style" very congenial to my own feelings, and to the feelings of those whom I have to consult, and I was doing too right to cavil or take offence.

We arrived at the place of destination to dinner, and the first delight of beholding the loveliest features of nature lighted up under a summer's sun, carriedus on tolerably through the meal; but scarcely was it concluded, when I found that I had a most humoursome being to deal with, whom all the blandishment and gentle endeavours of his suffering wife, could not soothe. Reading prayers myself to our little household before retiring for the night, he affected to be piqued at my supposed forgetfulness of his sacerdotal character, and desired me to leave that office to him. I did so on the following morning, and then it was not agreeable, nor was it ever after demanded. The striking of two clocks had disturbed his night's repose, and he ordered them to be stopped; the. embrace the doctrines of Christianity, with all their probing qualities, rather than to take refuge in breakfast-hour of nine required too long fasting; tea was carried to the chamber.

At breakfast, however, I had the happiness to hear that I gave satisfaction in all points but the dinner-hour, which postponed too long his " classic walk;" it was of no importr ance to ourselves, therefore cheerfully altered to an earlier hour. But my obedience displeased! O dear! dear! why did I mind what *he* said? He would not walk.

"May I help you, Sir, to a bit of this pie?" said some one.

"What is it?"

"Pigeon-pie."

"O, no, no! —That's too bilious for *me*. If it had been *giblet-pie* I should have liked it, — *that's* a nice dish!"

Two ladies came from Richmond to make an evening-visit

— a return of it, as they were women of taste, was approved and promised.

I pass over the hourly annoyance of repeated complaint, of habitual discontent, and manners subject to no bridle. The giblet-pie came according to the hint given. I believe in *that* instance shame in some degree interfered: "O dear! dear! it's very hard that I can't say what I like—well! give me some of it— very nice, upon my word." The palate was propitiated

— this was enough.

Our books were a natural resource. He had sold his libraryin confidence of having the use of another;—he was now bookless "he meant that each friend of his should give him a book — we had a very good collection of such books as he should most want, — Leunclavius's Xenophon, in particular." We were not such geese as to cackle in reply.

I 6 "The *r* obduracy, scepticism, or the delusive occupation of cultivating schism. And happy is it for us who

The evening for the visit came: when all was arranged, and it was too late to send an apology with any decency, my guest stood firm, and declared he would not go to be made a show in his disgrace. I had no choice—I submitted— trusting t telling the truth as my excuse.

Unfortunately one morning while we were at breakfast, a servant whispered the arrival of the fishmonger. "Now," said the visitor," let *me* see the fish and choose." All this had now become merriment, and I acquiesced willingly, but with secret resolves against future exposures to similar liberties.

I hope the reader sees us standing together by the well arranged fish-tray — I waited the "first turn" of my guest — "That pair of soals for me," said he; " take *them* for me—now you may buy what you like for the family." I obeyed, and would have done so had he ordered me to buy the tray itself, and send it up with anchovy-sauce.

We were now drawing to an end of the promised week, which I ought to have premised, was to be only of six days, —

"No joy shall last;" and it being a glorious time of year with seasonable weather, to be rowed down the river, and landed amongst those persons of fashion and distinction who came to listen to a band of music, was an attractive occupation of part of an evening. Every thing being ordered for this gay purpose, the moody man, on being summoned to the shore, stood there like one of Charon's reluctant passengers, arguing on the cruelty of taking him into a crowd, where every third person would know him, to expose him to the public gaze, and to meet and be met by questioners. I waited the adjustment of the balance i remain, that he has not lent his name to any fallacious opinions or convenient tenets. Whatever might be the vacillation or inconsistency of his opinions on other points, we are certain that one of the very first men that this country has to it paused at "acquiescence," and we arrived safe on this enchanted ground. I will not depart from the truth, nor resort to imagination to supply the want of recollection. I forget how I was tormented for this sin, but I recollect that all fears of celebrity proved unfounded. A voluntary signification of an intention to favour us again at Christmas, was given in good time before the hour of adieu arrived; the interval was to be filled up by visits to various friends, who were *clamorous* for the distinction of being kind in adversity, and whose letters of appointment were daily asked for, without arriving.

Christmas drew near, a morning-visit of reminding was made: it occurred when I was almost on my feet to go into London with a friend, whose carriage waited. The opportunity of an easy return was then supposed to have presented itself, almost by miracle; but the staying for this purpose proved ineffectual. A letter came next, intimating some disappointment and fear of having offended; a civil reply was made, but no invitation for Christmas added: —

"Hinc illae lachrymse."`

And hence spouted out words that needed repentance, preceding an attestation to character surreptitiously obtained; and the basis of which ought to have been better established than on the death-bed scenery, and *ipse dixit* of such a *moribond.* boast, and a man whose moral writings have obtained for him a rank which would have gratified the pride of an ancient philosopher, believed without compulsion, without the leading of interest, or the formalities of a profession, without exception or reservation, that the Almighty made and governs the world; that mankind have fallen from grace by sin; that there is no mean of recovering the Divine favour but through the merits of our Redeemer; that our own best endeavours, though not to. be neglected for a moment, must ever be found imperfect; and that the deepest contrition and sincerest repentance are as strictly required of the first of the human species, as of the lowest of the people.

The religious awe which overspread his mind was genuine, it was excessive, it was painful even to witness; and it deprived him of all the consolations of our faith. To imitate him in this point might lead to error; our peace of mind is to be established between God and ourselves, and not under the influence of any example in our own nature. Happy would it be for many, were they equally oppressed by it; and thrice happy are those, who, by a more fortunate and regular course of early life, have been led into the paths of peace, before the mind has been corroded by evil, and made restive by perverse habits.

That sorry professor of Christianity, Burns, whose daily practice was ever at war with his solitary meditations, but on whose mental vision seemed forced the great truths of religion, has almost involuntarily borne his testimony in favour of the adoption of those weighty sentiments, from which, alas! he took refuge in the lowest vices of the vulgar. His wild starts of religious poetry give us flashes of truth, which meet the conviction and experience of us all. Most truly does he say, and I wish the inconsiderate would go to him to learn more, —

— " when on life we're tempest-driven, A conscience but a canker,
A correspondence fix'd with heaven
Is sure a noble anchor."

It is some degree of forbearance to resume my own train of far inferior thought, in preference to quoting from this eccentric poet, some of the many beautiful passages in which his heart and pen have done honour to the Being, whom his too frequent submission to low temptations was almost daily offending. But here let us be charitable in the apostle's sense of the word. Let us, in contemplating the character, not only of Johnson, but of such as are endowed like Burns and live no better, recollect the doctrineof one of his best stanzas:—

"Who made the heart 'tis he alone
Decidedly can try us;
He knows each chord, its various tone,
Each spring, its various bias:
Then at the balance let's be mute,
We never can adjust it;
What's done we partly may compute,
But know not what's resisted."

And let us, who may sometimes repine at not having shared in the elevating talents of genius, duly consider their alloy, and how many painful conflicts we are spared, by feeling no opposition to the steady pursuit of our best interests. That, in Johnson's great mind, the conflict between his sense of right and his propensity to offend against that sense, was severe, does not rest on *me* to point out. It can surprise none but those who know not the bulk of such a mind, and the more than human force requi-

site to prevent its irrecoverable disobedience to the helm of conscience. But to that court he seems never to have summoned those petty offences which made him only disagreeable; and which would, if he could so have transgressed, have made the *un-irritable* but more susceptible Bennet Langton have walked half through London, had he on reflection seen any cause to apprehend that the lowest of its inhabitants had suffered pain from what had escaped his lips.

By the way, it is matter of curiosity to consider, *en passant,* the very different characters of four men living in an intimacy, which, according to the old adage, should have afforded a key to the sentiments of each; and if we take tenderness of conscience as the test of resemblance, we shall soon see the failure of the proverb as universally applied. Under the reminiscences of this troublesome visitant, Johnson groaned. Langton, at the least whisper of her gentle voice, went out to meet her: he asked what was her behest, and bowed down to the ground. Boswell, when he felt her whipcord, began vowing and protesting against her just remarks, but substituting other points, in making good which she might herself have failed: while Steevens would undauntedly have denied *in toto* all she could have said, and looking on his nearest neighbour, might have diverted the pursuit from himself, by the direction of his finger, and a whisper of that most hackneyed of all trite quotations, " *Hie niger."*

Much has been said of Johnson's superstitious scrupulosity; but it appears to me, with very little of just reference to the state of his mind. Could he have advanced with any confidence towards that happy calmness, in which, firm in principles and regular in practice, we begin to feel that the service required by the Gospel is the most perfect freedom, he would, I doubt not, have discarded this scrupulous and perpetually thwarted succession of attempts, and might have been at ease. But this was not ordained to be his lot: his natural infirmities were second causes, powerfully acting against his peace; but they render

his courageous returns to the attack, more worthy of applause; and it is still to be remarked, that he divested himself as far as he could, of mean assistances. He had given up wine, and there was not that growing indulgence of palliatives in his management of himself, into which many have fallen.

In his wish to leave nothing undone, he certainly attached too much importance to small things. In this minuteness he resembled a painter, who leaving the likeness of a portrait to take its chance, in despair of hitting it, should spend his time and efforts upon hair and curls. f And the short repetitions of his temporary severities were not unlike the compelled attention of a reluctant arithmetician, who afraid of encountering a new series of figures, goes back to repeat the process which requires no farther care. The use of Ether is little noticed, but its prevalence requires some check. Where it is *necesiary,* it would be very unreasonable to wish it disused, but the prodigal waste of it is with those who wish to raise their spirits, and who live upon them. I remember in my early days, a lady of great vivacity, whose approach when walking in St. James's Park was announced far off, and who with a very moderate income, was said to expend eighty-five pounds per annum in the most elegant species of this chemical preparation. f I cannot, in this train of thought, but recollect my father's words to me, when I once carried him some writing I had done, in which I had taken great pains to efface a word written twice over. He said, "If you had but taken as much care in writing as in effacing, you might have got more credit and commendation."

It was my business to select from his little books of self-examination, which came into my father's hands, the passages that should be printed as specimens; and I rejected, as subject to wild surmises, those which contained marks known only in their significations by himself.

He certainly considered the unbounded exercise of charity as atonement; and his almost indiscriminate application of it, proved that he added by every opportunity to his store. He always seemed to me in the situation of a man who, meaning well, but having never kept any accounts, gives up all that he has to spare, and adds his superfluities whenever they occur, to discharge debts, the amount of which he has never calculated.

That he should listen with little exhilaration of spirits to my father and others, who reminded him of the moral and religious tendency of his writings, I cannot think at all surprising. The dreadful waking, even in this life, to the sense of guilt, in having given to the world that which shall make it less deserving of its Creator, is a degree of horror not to be dwelt on; it must be beyond imagination: but the converse of this supposition is not in an equal degree soothing and consoling; nay, it is an argument that, when urged to us, must rather produce self-abasement, under the consciousness of the sad disproportion between our powers of enforcing precepts and practising them. Our divine bard did not write without thought or experience, when he told us that it is easier to teach twenty what is good, than to fulfil the duty of one of the twenty in practising the given lesson. But this must not discourage us, neither can it be brought in plea against the enormous crime of disseminating what is bad. Authors may write atrociously, and die witty, or senseless; but as we should not listen to any but the best evidence in seeking for truth, we are bound to believe the positive attestations borne to the end of some of these writers. Many may have been permitted to die in a state that "gives no sign." God only knows his own purposes, and punishment is not the less heavy for being secret; but *our* guide is the testimony of those who have been in a state to afford room for conclusions.

When Rousseau, who was branded with the reproach of having "a hankering after Christianity," was taunted with the supposition, that had he known Fenelon, he would have been one of his disciples, his answer, "I would have been his footman," was worth pages of recantation which the next freak of his

mind might have retracted. And when the nurse who attended Voltaire in his last illness, refused to go to another patient till assured that the sick person was a Christian, we ask no farther attestation of the horrors with which his death was said to be attended.

It is, however, curious, that these two evil spirits, and it is difficult to say which of them has brought most evil into the world, were of such different characters and opinions, that they could indulge in mutual abuse, and make profitable merriment for those who abhorred the one and loathed the other. Baron Grimm has given at length, in his Correspondence and Miscellaneous Collections, the sham prophetic review which Voltaire wrote of the Nouvelle Eloise; and it requires the recollection of his own atrocities to keep in our memory the conviction that the critic was as deserving of thorough disapprobation as the author. The whole of it would be tedious to the English reader, who may have lost all interest in the work, and parts of it are as gross as the subject of the review; but I have more than one aim in translating some of the clauses of it.

"About this time there will appear an extraordinary man, arrived from the border of a lake. He will cry out to the multitude, 'I am possessed by the demon of enthusiasm: I have received from Heaven the gift of inconsistency: I am a philosopher, and a professor of paradox.'

"And the multitude will run after him, and many will give credit to him.

"And he will say, 'You are all rascals and rogues: your women are all profligate, and I am coming to live among you.'

"And he will abuse the good-nature of these people, that he may calumniate them.

"And he will tell them that all the people in the country where he was born, are virtuous, and that he never could live in the country of his birth.

"And he will maintain that arts and sciences corrupt the mind, and he will write on them all.

"And he will condemn the theatre as

the school of vice, and write dramatic pieces for it.

"And he will maintain, that the uncivilised are the virtuous, though he knows nothing of them, but is most fit for their society.

"And he will say that all people of rank are contemptible, and he will accept all the invitations of persons of rank when invited to be *shown off*

"And he will say, that nobody who reads romances can have any morals, and he will write a romance, and in it he will exhibit vice in actions, and virtue in words, and his personages will be crazy with love and philosophy.

"And in his romance he will teach the art of philosophic seduction.

"And his pupil will lose all sense of shame and decency, and will talk nonsense and maxims with her instructor.

"And all the book will be moral, useful, and decorous — and it will prove, that provided young women are always talking of virtue, they are under no necessity of practising it.

"And the pupil will declare, that affection between married persons is misplaced; and she will undertake to prove it, and fancy she has done sq.

"And the book will be written in an imposing style, in order to delude silly people.

"And the author will make his own phrases, and take them for arguments.

"And like all quacks, who make wounds on purpose to show the healing quality of their balm, he will poison the minds of his readers, to have the credit of curing them; and the poison will act violently on their hearts, and his antidote only on the mind, so that the poison will have the upper hand.

"And he will boast of having led them to a precipice; and will think himself blameless, because he has warned his readers in a preface, knowing that young people never read prefaces.

"And after he has, in his romance, degraded in their turn, morals by his philosophy, and philosophy by his morals, he will say, that romances are indispensably necessary to a corrupt people.

"And he will likewise say, to justify himself in having written a work highly immoral, that he lives in an age when it is impossible to be good.

"And to excuse himself, he will lay the blame on the universe.

"And he will threaten with his displeasure those who do not approve his book."

I have said, that I had more than one view in bringing forward these sentences. I have lost my labour, if the reader does not perceive that the wit of Voltaire might, with little omission or alteration, be applied to some of the productions of the present day. Substitute religion, such as it is in these works, for philosophy, such as it was in those which have done such subtle mischief, and, I believe, the resemblance will come out. And I look on some of *our* productions as still worse than the former race, because we *may* read, and we *must* read perhaps half a volume, before we are awake to the soil on which we are treading; — they appear not only innocent, but virtuous, and even religious!

It is worth the trouble to trace cursorily the fashion of light reading, from a period which many can recollect — that period, when the very coarse writers were put out of sight; when chambermaids and washerwomen, who had before been accepted as the conductors of the *interests* of young ladies, were thought fit acquaintance for none but eloping hoydens and intriguing romps ; and when persons of any discrimination, I had almost said of common decency, (and I know not why I should not say it,) began to loathe Pamela. The world then grew more tolerant of Grandison, whose surfeit of I foresee I shall have the Sosia, the Parmeno, and Geta of Terence quoted against me as the archetypes of the gentlewomen whose services I so depreciate. I will not be unjust, but two thousand years make some alterations, with which it is not only prudent, but incumbent on us, to comply.

manners had partially injured him when his novelty was over.

But Clarissa held her place through all the variations of fashion. The coffin and white satin were the license; the brothel and the beastliness conducted to

them, and therefore must be a fair way. Rousseau was decent compared to Richardson; yet abstracts were made from Clarissa, and put into the hands of children! I never can forget that when I was about ten years old, I had heard these works commended by visitors and very much decried by my mother. I, of course, set her opinion down in my own catalogue of those prejudices, which could be designed for nothing but to keep *us* in subjection, and ignorant of all that delighted others; the catalogue I confess was long, A lady of a very long memory, and who adds to her own intelligent recollections those of her mother, tells me that she had often heard her say, that the manners with which Richardson endows his personages, were no more those of the time when he wrote, than they are of our own time. The same I have heard from others; and whatever the enthusiastic admirers of his writings may endeavour to prove, there is every indication in them, that it was to them that he owed his introduction to persons of a rank above him.

and had been considered quite sufficiently, when fortune seemed to offer me some relief. Shame to say! from a day-school, kept by two worthy women, who with the rest of the world admired Richardson, I brought home, as a valuable loan, this Lilliputian volume of the "concentrated essence" of the divine Clarissa. Sanctioned by the reputable means of obtaining this treasure, I used no concealment; nay, I even thought I should bring father and mother over to the general opinion, and assist in making them, what I much wished them to be, "more like other people." It may be *supposed* that it was a purified edition of the work which I had obtained; but on my announcing it, my mother begged to look at it. It had *pictures, tant mieux pour moi,* thought I,—I love pictures: and seriously it was *tant mieux,* though I at the next moment thought it *tant pis pour moi:* for my mother sparing no expressions of indignation, sent it back with a message of supposition that the transaction had been clandestine.

Long after, when my father, then sure

of my taste, and taking off his prohibition as to my reading, advised me not to remain entirely ignorant of books on which I might be expected to form an opinion, I availed myself of a friend's library and got through many volumes; but when my friend lent me Clarissa, I returned it so soon, as to excite enquiries as to my fair dealing; I con-' fessed the truth: I had read only the heads of the chapters! Richardson or his editor is most liberal in this species of whetstone to curiosity; but the sample satisfied me. I was not however so let off; I was forced to plunge into the Stygian stream, and my disgust was dyed in grain.

Astonished was I, when I found the *men* the advocates of Clarissa, and dating their habits of virtue from their acquaintance with it. To a female ear such a declaration was almost affronting. "I caught you asleep and stole a pair of gloves," is an old-fashioned form of country-jocularity, not by many degrees so mortifying as the consciousness of the exposures of loose writers, amongst whom I do not scruple to number Richardson, notwithstanding all his sentimentality.

Whoever has perused that really valuable publication, Richardson's Correspondence, must recollect the enthusiastic devotion of Lady Echlin; yet she, in all her fervour, thought proper to write to him in these words, which may be found in vol. v. p. 54.

"I am even ill-natured enough to wish that, whenever you are disposed to write again, you would disappoint your readers, by not making the passion of love their entertainment. Allow me to say, *the finest lessons you have written, and the best instruction you can give, blended with love-intrigues, will never answer your good intentions."*

What would Lady Echlin say now, when *love-intrigues,* in their simple mode of existence, might be referred to as comparatively harmless?

Unaccustomed to read much for amusement, and never having an hour of which I wished to get rid, I must make a long step over the novels of various authors, to come down to the exemplary endeavours of several who preceded but a little, the "Ccelebs" of our first female advocate for the union of religion with morality. This work, new in its kind, attractive in its language, lively in its tone, seemed to form an epocha in moral fiction, and procured favour for others which had the same motive to plead; and nothing was for a time admissible into the *boudoir* or the school-room, but that which had a moral.

I was, for some years, very intimately acquainted with a barrister of eminence, for the regularity of whose life, the strictness of whose morals, and the sincere piety of whose character, I thought I could have been responsible. He was much with us, and delighted in the society of our house; and I know no point in which we disagreed, but our opinion of Richardson: still I excused his sentiments, because he gave his approbation solely to that which is liable to no objection but its proximity to evil; yet the consciousness of the dirt through which he had waded, tacitly destroyed all idea of delicacy, or his disgust at the want of it. We parted never to meet again! then was revealed such a course of turpitude as I cannot describe.

For God's sake! let us never so deceive ourselves. If we have proceeded so far as not to know right from wrong, let us go back to the Prophets, the Gospels, and St. Paul; there is no compounding.

We are sometimes astonished by a second choice that is unwise, when a first has been wise. Who could have imagined that all this preference of good should have left the taste of those early trained in it, open to the reception of fantastic effusions of poetry, bringing forward under a disguise not of texture enough to be called a veil, mixtures of religion, immorality, and profaneness, so blended as to puzzle, perplex and mislead, and defying excision because indissolubly connected with that which must be admired?

That a taste for the innocent marvellous should have discouraged all attempts at moral improvements, is hardly to be mentioned after such a statement. In *that* department we are but in the

situation from which Cervantes rescued his countrymen ; but there are writers who are trying in various ways what the town will bear, some by a mixture of nationality, enthusiasm, and sensuality, perfectly entrapping; and when we object to such strong painting of the steps by which the once exemplary have descended into the abyss of wickedness, we are asked whether that abyss is not its own punishment; and we are told that every one, *such* by nature and cultivation, and *so* circumstanced, must have acted in the same manner. f I do not wish to say any thing against the monopoly of the public attention, by writers so universally admired as those who make history subservient to fiction; but I believe I meet the wishes of many, if I protest against giving to any human being, the awful title of The Great Unknown. I might perhaps surprise by the question, " Do you know what you are doing?" t I was entrapped by a very worthy young friend, into reading the memoirs of a Scotch pastor; who through pure morbid feeling was seduced into a shameful intercourse, by a woman whose very outset rendered her suspected. My friend t considered the subsequent contrition and suffering as giving the work every right to acceptance; and so it might, but I sickened in the middle of the elaborate description of approximation; and the meretricious character of its

Some few years have now elapsed, since one of our popular writers, whose works have now acquired great reputation, expressed the greatest disgust at the morbid evil of the then fashionable works of imagination, and his toleration of the grossness of the old school in preference to it, and he was right; inasmuch as the danger which gives us warning, is less than that which steals on us insidiously. What he has to say of that school and its productions which has sprung up under the dissemination of new doctrines, I know not; but I think had he heard some of the apologetical oratory of reasoners, who think nothing short of laying bare to the bone a cure for our maladies, he would ere now have cried out again.

To connect what I have here said with the character of Johnson, I would ask any one to consider the immense weight which he would have felt on his mind in his latter days, had it been only as they approached, that he betook himself to useful writing. The reception his Rasselas met with, might have encouraged an author to rest on his imagination, and deal in airy fiction, without much regard to the moral of his fable. But whatever cause Johnson had for his deep contrition, it is not to be found in the productions of his pen. He might at one time be a hot-headed politician, and, as he describes himself, after a houseless night he might shake hands with Savage in a resolution " to stand by the country;" he might make his political prejudices ply under the pressure of his necessities: but this was trifling compared with the heinous offence of insinuating the worst principles in the best verse; exciting those passions which we are commanded to keep under; rendering familiar scenes of atrocity; or purchasing the privilege to describe adultery by *innuendo,* with an undertaking to prove that a reconciling penitence followed. What if there were "no place for repentance?" "Hazard not thyself in the shadow of corruption," is, I think, one of the authoritative injunctions of that deep thinker and brief reasoner, Sir Thomas Browne; and surely the opinion of those whom the world has long ago agreed to denominate "the wise," is better worth listening to than the airy notions of those who have yet to take their rank in estimation, and who, writing under the influence of voluntary intoxication, stand little chance of acquittal in the court of the sober.

most saintly passages affronted me. Our Blessed Lord has truly said, "He that is not for me is against me;" and such works certainly are not written on *his* side of the greatest question that can be tried.

I perceive that I have said nothing of Johnson's great work, his Dictionary. It was omitted for that best of all good reasons, that I had nothing to say, unless that I wonder that any body should have wondered at Dr. Robertson's saying that he had read it all through. To be read through, is, in my opinion, its best purpose, as it is a body of evidence on the pretensions of the individual words of the language. Excepting the authority we give it, I do not think it is more a directory in lexicography, that his Lives of the Poets are in criticism. "The world" is very much " before us" in both. Bailey's Dictionary is a more decidedly useful book of reference.

But in the case of a Scotch writer, assiduous to perfect an English style, the value of the work is much enhanced. It is confessed by themselves, that in writing for "the Southrons," they write a language not their own; how *well* they can write for " the Southrons," is made pretty clear, and was early demonstrated by this patient peruser of our national dictionary.

If I attempt to atone for omissions, I may indulge in speaking of Johnson's editing the "Christian Morals" of Sir Thomas Browne, which appears to me to have left a very strong and a permanent influence on his habits of thinking, or of expressing his thoughts — so strong, that I wonder it has not been more dwelt on. As to *my good father,* he seems to me to have passed over the circumstance, or it is omitted in the index — Pr. Mackie, for many years the principal physician at Southampton, a man with whom it *was,* and I hope I may still say *is,* my happiness to be acquainted, made a visit to Edinburgh, where he had previously placed his son under Professor Dalziel, at a point of time when the Professor lay dying. Dr. Mackie expressing his anxiety to do something for his relief, he declared his case hopeless, adding, "You see me on a classic bed, —here Robertson expired." the very worst index I ever saw, and not, I can assure the reader, of *my* making.

But whatever the omission, I cannot omit to record as an obligation conferred on the world, this introduction to popular favour, of a work perhaps little known at the time, and T am sorry to say, not as much known, even now, as it deserves to be, or as our needs require. Lord Bacon's Essays the work I now mention, and Felltham's Resolves, with

the Scriptures and our Liturgy, Bishop Patrick's Christian Sacrifice, and Bishop Andrews's Devotions, form the library which I should present to any friend quitting this country. Other books may be procured, and amusements are ever attainable in a foreign land; but these are the works which will best keep us steady in our moral duties, raise our minds in that progression of improvement which we ought to demand of ourselves, and contribute to return us to the regular offices of our church, without the painful consciousness that we have lost way in the pursuit of pleasure, knowledge, or worldly advantage.

My father has saved me the trouble and necessity of remarking on the implicit credit due to Johnson's expressions of fondness for his wife while she lived, and of sorrow for her death. There are in the world some persons whom hardly the sight of a parish-register would make those who know them believe *married.* Their habits are so *single,*-their whole appearance and deportment show so little of conformity to any taste but their own; there is about them so insulated an indifference, so unconnected, so unreferring a recoil into themselves, that I have known fifty years not sufficient to impress on the belief of others, the fact of their being in the list of *couples.* Had Mrs. Johnson even outlived her husband, he must have remained in this situation of disbelief; and where those feelings were lodged that fermented so violently on the demise of this comical sort of a wife, which dissolved this incongruous union, my father has left, and I must still leave, every one to guess. He might, in the deep tones of his conscience, in the tenderness of which, would to God we could all imitate him! take to himself blame for the little cultivation he had, at one period, given to domestic comfort; he might, in solitude, feel that even that which he had at times lightly prized, had value; he might feel his melancholy — most pitiable melancholy! made heavier by losing even that person, whose presence often teased him; he might feel painfully that near approach of death which is hinted by a week's

abode with the dead; but the *kitten-ing,* the *Tetty-ing,* and all this contemptible puerility, is to the last degree unaccountable.

What the ceconomy of Dr. Johnson's house might be under this administration I cannot tell; but under Mrs. Williams's management, and indeed afterwards, when he was even more at the mercy of those around him, it always exceeded my expectations, as far as the condition of the apartment into which / was admitted, could enable me to judge. It was not, indeed, his study, amongst his *books,* he probably might bring Magliabecchi to recollection; but I saw him only in a decent drawing-room of a house not inferior to others in the same local situation, and with stout old-fashiOned mahogany chairs and tables. I have said, that he was a liberal customer to his tailor; and I can remember, that his linen often was a strong. contrast to the colour of his hands. In truth, I think he must have had much the advantage of Voltaire, in the good sense shown in that which met so unobtrusively the eye of an observer. Perhaps the reader would forgive a short digression to preserve the recollection of a visit made to " the philosopher of Ferney," in the year 1763, by Count Jarnac, whom I shall more fully introduce to the reader hereafter. This nobleman being then stationed with his regiment at Schlestat in Alsace, and having early acquired a literary taste, had a great inclination to make a visit to Ferney. He therefore sent over a message requesting permission to pay his respects to Monsieur de Voltaire, which was returned by profound acknowledgments of the honour, and the appointment of a day and hour, with an invitation to dine. The affairs of France were then such as admitted of the observances of rank; and the Count, whose pride was English horses and carriages, went in his proper style, taking with him the officer next in command to him, and a friend. They arrived at Ferney about noon, and found Voltaire sitting, though it was in a very hot July, by a great fire, drest in a large wig, over which he wore a cap of embroidered blue velvet; he had on him a night-gown of rich brocade, a magnificent waistcoat, roll-up stockings and slippers. He professed himself highly gratified by the visit, but not even this feeling could keep out of sight the ill quality of his temper. Complaints of his own infirmities, and sarcastic expressions of ill will towards individuals, occupied much of his conversation; and in his wailings, he referred to something with which the Count was not then acquainted, by saying, "Ah! Monsieur! vous me traitez beaucoup mieux que M. voire pere m'a traite." This, the Count found afterwards, referred to a circumstance recorded in the anecdotes of Maurepas, and which had occasioned Voltaire's being sent for a time to the common gaol, and Monsieur de Rohan to the Bastille.

At about half past one, Voltaire made an excuse, saying he must go and dress, which, he observed, was not his daily custom, but a point of respect to his guests. He spoke of the sad lateness of hours, and deplored the necessity of following the mode, by dining so late as two o'clock.

His manner of speaking seemed to correspond with his manner of feeling. All that he said, instead of being on general or liberal topics, was a succession of querulous egotism; and they were delivered in a continued howl, accompanied by the oddest gesture that can be conceived—that of raising his elbows as high as his ears, joining his fingers, and "sawing the air," if the reader can understand by this, a horizontal movement backwards and forwards, repeating, "Ah! ah! le vieux malade, — ah! je suis le vieux malade, — ah! vous voyez le vieux malade."

In his absence, the visitors were left to the benevolence of Madame Denys, who, to the last degree homely, seemed a party in all the concerns of the seigneur du chateau. She talked incessantly of the writings of Voltaire, and in speaking of them, named herself as if a sharer in his labours, using the plural in her little details: "Quand nous avians ji-ni le Mahomet, &c."

The dinner-party was only the three visitors, the master of the house,

Madame Denys, and a young female of the name of Crebillon, the most insipid of all insipid damsels, but whom Voltaire seemed ready to worship, as a descendant, I suppose a grand-daughter, of the celebrated writer. The dinner was good; the fish was the delicate ombre chevalier, or more correctly, umble chevalier, from the lake of Geneva.

After dinner, Voltaire led his guests round his potagerie to the place which he had prepared for his interment, which was a pyramidal sarcophagus. Under this, the earth was dug away to receive the coffin. But the whole seriousness of the business was converted into puerility; and the whole credit due to so close a consideration of the end of human life, was rendered something below even hypocrisy, by his exulting, as he exhibited the edifice, in the fruitlessness of the erection. He raised his elbows, sawed the air, and with a sort of chuckling, if so low an expression may be admitted, repeated to himself, "Ah! ah! but they will never let me lie here, they will have me to Paris I know."

The Count concluded his little memoir with his own opinion, that had his host rested quiet at Ferney, while alive, he would as quietly have taken possession of his cemetery; but he went to Paris, as if to verify his prediction.

I have hinted, that as Johnson lost his original associations, he assumed new ones. To those friends with whom my father first knew him, succeeded those who felt themselves raised in the republic of belles lettres, by the having him to boast of, as an addition to the attractions of their elegant tables; and if these failed him, he was sometimes to be found in odd corners, where least looked for. I remember once meeting him in a very strange one.

My mother had received a visit from a little old blind lady, who introduced herself under the supposition that we were Sir Csesar Hawkins's family. She was of the noble family of Howard, and had married into that of Hervey. She was living in a state of separation from her husband; and the wildness of her conversation, the eccentricity of her modes of life, and the singular incon-

gruities of her habiliments, for dress they could hardly be called, increased at every interview, doubts of the soundness of her mind. She generally harboured somewhere in the neighbourhood of Pimlico; and, being very desirous of attentions, This was consistent with bis advice to others.

/ received them from Lady H., who wished as far as she had influence, to keep those about the old lady awake to the services she required. In an evening-visit which she exacted from my mother, we found her room filled by a few unconnected persons, and amongst them Dr. Johnson. Besides him, there was but one male visitor, a very modest clergyman, who was well disposed to listen without any. pretension to contradict. The conversation was very much between my mother and Dr. Johnson; and I recollect then first learning, and from him, what was the average quantity of rain that falls in England.

At the conclusion of this visit, Johnson desired my mother to take him home with her; and he finished his evening with my father, who, rather surprised at hearing where he had been picked The lady above mentioned had probably possessed some brilliancy of intellect. She talked of persons of a former generation, with perfect recollection, and I remember her making herself very merry, with the upstart pride of a man of the name of Howard, just then trying his fortune in medicine, and who, on launching his carriage, sent to Norfolk House, to learn of the Duke himself, what tailor was employed to make the family-liveries.

up, enquired of him what motive could induce him to come so far from home, on such an invitation. He had nothing to plead for it, but the means it afforded of getting rid of an evening. It is a trifle to observe on, but it shows that Johnson was not inattentive to trifles, that before he desired Lady H. to afford him a conveyance, he had the consideration to ask her, seeing that she was not unaccompanied, whether her carriage was a coach or a chariot.

I might have remarked in a fitter place, on the disposition which Johnson has sometimes shown, even in print, to make neat compliments; and very neat they often are, exhibiting a mind free from all jealous seizure on importance, and most candidly turning the light from himself to another. His Scotch tour abounds with these gems of equity; and he prefaces the Life of Young with one of his best specimens. In his colloquial intercourse they were studied, and therefore lost their effect: his head dipped lower; the semicircle in which it revolved was of greater extent; and his roar was deeper in its tone when he meant to be civiL His movement in reading, which he did with great rapidity, was humorously described after his death, by a lady, who said that his head "swung seconds."

The usual initial sentences of his conversation led some to imagine that to resemble him was as easy as to mimic him, and that, if they began. with " Why, Sir," or " I know no reason," or " If any man chooses to think," or "If you mean to say," they must of course " talk Johnson." That his style might be imitated is true, and that its strong features made it easier to lay hold on it than on a milder style, no one will dispute.

For the following trifling circumstances connected with Dr. Johnson, I am indebted to my younger brother: they may be important only as connected with a man, all whose words have been considered as worthy of preservation. *(Loquitur H. H.)*

"Speaking of reading and study, I heard him say that he would not ask a man to give up his important interests for them, because it would not be fair; but that if any man would employ in reading that time which he would otherwise waste, he would answer for it, if he were a man of ordinary endowments, that he would make a sensible man. 'He might not,' said he, 'make a Bentley, but he would be a sensible man.'

It is very much to be regretted that he did not carry into effect his intention of translating Plutarch's Lives, as well as that he did not proceed in his imitations of Juvenal.

He was adverse to departing from the common opinions and customs of the world, as conceiving them to have been founded on experience.

He doubted whether there ever was a man who was not gratified by being told that he was liked by the women.

He was speaking of surgical operations. I suggested that they were now performed with less pain than formerly, owing to modern improvements in science. 'Yes, Sir,' said he, 'but if you will conceive a wedge placed with the broad end downwards,' alluding to the drawing of a tooth, 'no human power, nor angel, as *I* conceive, can extract that wedge without giving pain.'

He spoke contemptuously of the habit of cor

L responding by letter, and of professing to *pour out one's soul* upon a sheet of paper.

Calling upon him shortly after the death of Lord Mansfield, and mentioning the event, he answered, 'Ah! Sir, there was little learning and less virtue.'

Upon my mentioning that Mr. Harris of Salisbury had said that Akenside's Ode to Hastings was the finest ode in our language, he cried out, ' Harris is a coxcomb.'"

I should regret that I did not use, in due time, the opportunities which I had of knowing more of Johnson. But here I am carried back, as I have ever found myself, to my original feeling. No advantage that I could have gained, would have induced me to risk his rude asperity; I should have sunk under, or rather I should have been blown to atoms by, one of his concentrated explosions of contradiction; and I know of no claim that I had to mercy.

Of this feeling I allow no one to judge who has not been brought up, as I was, under "the depressing system," a system I cannot recommend, however *wholesome* it may I was content to view him, as I would a wild beast, at a due distance, and always with a retreat in my power. But that he was not without some degree of concern for me, I have to boast. Our friend Mrs. Welch was not always satisfied with the quantity of indulgence allowed me: she thought I should suffer, on my entrance on the world, by that in which I had no choice;

and she consulted him on the propriety of interference. He said "No: be quiet,—the child will never be blamed for the system of its parents." And in a case in which she thought my father made a wrong decision, she again consulted him, and getting his opinion on her side she protested against the proceeding, and backed her remonstrance by avowing the appeal she had made.

It would be absurd to compare Johnson and my father, either in natural endowments or in the degrees of acquired knowledge. But I feel no am ultimately prove. It is not *very* pleasant to fancy one's self, for perhaps nearly half one's life, utterly good for nothing; but it is greatly conducive to the security and satisfaction of the latter half, by fencing us against many vexations, by giving a zest to every rational pleasure, and making every kindness doubly felt.

bitious regret that I cannot boast myself the daughter of Johnson. To have been the daughter of a man whose mind habitually, even from his earliest youth, preferred "whatsoever things are pure and of good report;" whose pursuits and associations were such as he could not only excuse, but might have exulted in; who made the most of his talents for his own fair advantage and the benefit of the world; and whose greatest faults, I believe, were some degree of prejudice and stiffness of opinion, which opinion was in itself seldom wrong in its foundation, is to me far greater happiness, than any inherited celebrity: and had I been called to witness such a death-bed conflict as that of his friend, I know nothing that could have consoled me.

My father got a considerable quantity of abuse, absolutely as if he had meant to purloin a jewel, for his caution in keeping out of sight one little book in Johnson's writing, which was of a more private nature than the rest. I really believe Johnson's best friends were suspicious of Boswell; for I know it was a matter agreed with Mr: Langton, nay, which he himself suggested, thatnothing should be left in his way to examine. My father considered confessions made to our Maker, his ministers, or ourselves, as sacred, and was not so enthusiastically ingenuous as to approve the laying open the thoughts of a friend, who shared in the common infirmities of human nature, to a world in the corrupt state of that in which we live. Mr. Boswell, on the contrary, would have told any thing he could get at; and his revelations have pleased.

The biography of Johnson's in-door and outof-door patients would have been a display not at all tending to raise his character for prudence. Mrs. Williams was by far the most decent of the set; but different stages were occupied by persons whom his wild benevolence alone kept in sight. Of these some, even long after his death, hung heavy on the purses of his friends, merely on the pretension of having been known as pensioners of Dr. Johnson's.

But there was one man in particular, who ought to have been better remembered in his will, and yet was totally omitted. This was Humphry Heely, who had been distantly allied to him by marriage, and who was living with a second wife in an almshouse. I know it has been considered an offence of a heinous magnitude, to weigh any claim against the *merits* of Mr. Francis Barber, merits that had no foundation, but in his consultation of his own interest or the perverseness of his admirers; but unless Johnson had, when making his will, entirely lost all recollection of Heely, I know nothing that can excuse his petulant refusal to consider how the residue of his property should be disposed of. My father urged that and every other point of religious and moral obligation, with the gentleness of a divine, and the skill of a lawyer. He had only his own integrity to requite him.

The benevolent interest which Sir J. H. took in this man's pitiable condition made him cling very close to him; but his pretensions to regard are so fully detailed in The Life, that it would be superfluous to repeat them.

I never shall forget the first interview with him, which was to inform him of Dr. Johnson's neglect of him, and of the generosity of Mr. Langton and Lady Diana Beauclerk, in giving up, for the benefit of him and other persons, in the same predicament, that to which they had themselves a legal right. He had been a tall athletic hard-favoured man, labouring under the misfortune of great lameness from a contracted knee: his demeanor, though perfectly consonant to his low estate, had a liberal yeoman's character about it, that spoke of better days. He was the scathed oak of a former century: but a few arid symptoms of foliage testified that he had once been leafy.

I cannot, even at the distance of more than twenty-five years, read my father's narrative of this man's deplorable situation, without the painful feeling of sorrow for his hardships, and something little less than indignation at the barbarous apathy of Johnson, whose former assistance however capriciously afforded, must have excited hope that he should not be forgotten at his death. The terms in which he sometimes used to relieve him deserve comment. When Heely endeavoured to explain his wretched state of poverty, Johnson would not always hear him: he replied harshly, "You are poor, that's enough. " This avowal of indiscriminate feeling for all who could plead want, was not very consoling to such a mind as that of his pensioner, who was, as well as himself, a man of a very meditative cast. It put him undeservedly below that worthless being whom he smothered with ostentatious munificence, and eventually ruined by it.

All this indifference to the comfort of those whom he was to leave behind, convinces me, who can be actuated by no prejudice, that Johnson's charities were bribes to his mental and corporal disease; and that, beyond the lulling of his own desponding irritations, by the consciousness of fulfilling a duty, they had no purpose. It may be pleasant to those whose sympathy I may have excited, to assure them that the very silence of Johnson's will was construed into a loud call on the attention of our family. Paupers as Heely and his wife were, they maintained an idiot child, cast upon them by a stranger; and in all that was done for them, poor Peter was included. They knew no want while they lived, and at their death received decent interment. A worthy woman who had, early in the youth of my brothers and myself, come into the service of our family, attached herself strongly to them, and watched over them; and to the honour of servitude be it said, that when we lost my father, his man-servant presented Heely with one of his deceased master's suits of black, and every other article necessary for his decent appearance in mourning. Thus equipped and his wife not forgotten, they stood by the grave in the cloister of Westminster, and saw the remains of their benefactor committed to the earth. f

But I must not suffer it to appear as if these worthy people had made no requital. On the contrary, the utmost in their power was thought by them too little. Their alms-house had a pretty bit of garden: this was set with beans, raised solely for *me:* and that I might have them in perfection, they would rise at midnight to water them. They had a vine, and I fear their generous gratitude never permitted them to taste its fruit. And I may say, never was a funeral-sermon more expressive of the worth of a departed friend, than were Heely's broken sentences, when he first met us after the death of my father. His utterance was choked; but he strove to hush his feelings; and it seemed a recollection peculiarly grateful Jo them, that his best friend's last hour was the first of the day on which we *that* year commemorated the Ascension into Heaven, of Him on whom all our hopes rest.

The man's name was Richard Mason. He was a native of Ashby de la Zouch in Leicestershire. f A slip of paper found in my mother's desk on her demise, enjoined her children to do as she had done, for those to whom she had been kind. Her death occurred 1793; and the last of these personages died at the conclusion of 1823. They were fourteen in number; and to contrive for their comfort was the chief employment of her thoughts. The only difference ever made was by an equivalent composition, which change of residence made expedient. . Whether, of all Dr. Johnson's friends, my father was the most or the least competent to be his biographer, is a question which I am very willing to leave doubtful. Were I to vote on the subject, I should myself hesitate. Their friendship was indeed of long standing, and had therefore commenced sufficiently early to give Sir J. H. opportunity of studying his character under various lights: this, his powers enabled him to do on an enlarged scale.

The London booksellers certainly thought my father the fittest person, or they would not have sent a deputation to him, to ask him to undertake the labour. But I shall never cease to wonder at their doing so, for Boswell's views were, I think, suspected, if not declared; and unless he asserts as bold a falsity as in the story of Lady Rothes's It is very painful to be driven to use harsh expressions; but violations of truth cannot be treated too harshly; especially when we consider the increased latitude which those who have no regard for it assume, whenever they can quote the lenity used by others under this provocation, or palliate the crime by subdivision of lies into classes. I am obliged to look into both the lives to refresh my memory, and even now I may make mistakes; but I can safely say, it will not be from want of integrity or caution. One case of this assumption of bold falsity, I cannot pass over. Mr. Boswell says of that distressing circumstance, Johnson's endeavour to relieve himself from the pressure of dropsy, " This bold attempt, Sir J. H. has related in such a manner as to suggest a charge against Johnson of intentionally hastening his end." Now my father's words are these: "That this act was *not* done to hasten his end, but to discharge the water that he conceived to be in him, mango, he had at least tacit permission to exhibit him to the public: and it is very remarkable, and not in the common course of self-care, that notwithstanding this bare-faced *espionnage,* Johnson never appears to have been influenced in his conversation, either in matter or manner. He

J have not the least doubt." I make no comment; the atrocity of a falsehood so easy of detection, can excite only horror

and contempt in those who advert to the first principles of morals; but to the slippery consciences of those who can reply —" Ah well well!"—and "But, but you must consider," and " Allowance must be made,"—and "The world is not so strict," I make no appeal. I have heard of a lady at a card-table who was seen to take half a guinea out of the pool. A gentleman standing by said, "Ma'am, I certainly saw you take it out." "Did you, Sir?" she replied; " then now you may see me put it in again."—Perhaps this may be called repentance and restoration, / call it effrontery: and worse than effrontery, I denominate Boswell's conduct in this and other instances.

My father lived not to know how he had been traduced: but even had he survived the slanderer, he would have contented himself with making one passage confront the other: he would have made neither complaint nor appeal.

On the subject of being, as he called it, a woolpack under the attacks of malice, he was heartily joined by the frequent companion of his walks, the then Bishop of Bangor, who said, that were a paragraph to appear in the public papers, stating that the Bow Street Officers were in pursuit of him for a highway robbery, he would not take the pains to contradict it.

who professed to talk for victory, never appeared to talk for reputation. He certainly calculated, and very accurately, the angle at which what he uttered would do most execution; and those in the habit of hearing him, might, when he was well warmed in conversation, observe in him a concentration of his forces, when he meant to be decisive. I was ready to cry out, "Now for it," while I awaited these explosions, as I should have done, had I seen him inflate his cheeks to try how far he could blow a feather; and feathers indeed some speakers were before him.

But against all this, he who waited for the death of his friend with views that might bear a rude comparison, was proof. Why he was not present at the last scenes of this eventful life, was never clearly made out. There was a sort of coquetry in his absence, which was ex-

cused by the absentee, rather in the language of a lover than a friend; and it is no compliment to the character which he performed, that he does not appear to have been wanted or wished for. I do not think Johnson ever named him to my father.

But while I thus depreciate a man who really has done still more to depreciate himself, I would net be unjust to his work. His Life of Johnson is a book that must always please; it is entertaining to a degree that makes my father's appear stiff, cold, and turgid; and I cannot but own, I think my father's the very worst thing he ever gave to the public. That there was a time when he could have done much better, I will endeavour to prove, by producing in some future pages, specimens of his *own* style, as I should call it.

That the style in which he wrote Johnson's Life was not *his own,* is an opinion supported in my mind by the train of study into which he fell after he had completed his History of Music. He made the completion of that great labour an epocha in his own life; and, undisturbed, except by the trifling occupation of a new edition of the Complete Angler, to which at every call he was ready to lend his assistance, he was retreating to those books that best befitted his advancing period of life. These were the works of such men as Taylor, Barrow, Hooker, and others, who thought nothing said while any thing remained to be said. Besides this, he had imperceptibly imbibed their mode of using connective parts of speech which tend to heaviness, and consequently abate interest. Lives so differently written as the two under consideration, come into different classes of literary productions. If the world desire the *capillary* painting of the Dutch school, the Dutch artist is their proper painter. My father was a *devote* of Titian; Burke would have sketched with the masterly hand of Raffaelle; and the performances of the two latter, when conjointly contrasted with the former, would have exhibited the same difference as between representation and exposure: for I err grossly in judgment if I am wrong in thinking, that, in the hand of his unreserved biographer, Johnson is much lowered. His early deviations are detailed almost to grossness, his waywardness, his solicitude to please his palate, and all his faults, are as much in the foreground and sunshine, as his highest virtues. All is told, and all has been well received, as giving a full meal to inquisitiveness; and nothing less than the satisfaction of prying curiosity has been accepted, since this feast was afforded.

But were this excess of exposure to be the general plan of life-writing, much of the benefit of example would be lost. We may fairly hope to have our height measured when we stand upright; we do not ask for stilts or high heels; we expect only to have our powers estimated by an average: but if this *commerage* is necessary to biography, I think we must leave an injunction in our wills against such recording. There are not many who would not be degraded by it. A few words of Sir Isaac Newton's, are treasures; but who would care to be told that he was enraged at a bad stage-coach dinner, unless they wished him reduced to a lower level of estimation than that by nature allotted him. Sir J. H. has descended too low in recording the French duck-pie and pheasant eaten, almost *in extremis;* but very very probably *I* might stickle for its insertion in a mischievous relish of the contrasted circumstances. Who is not ready to cry " Shame, shame, silence!" when they read the squabbling between one of the first men of his time, and one of the finest gentlemen of his class, as were Johnson and Beauclerk, on the question whether a suicide should take one or two pistols for his purpose? It is downright brutal ill manners. I wonder whether Johnson really could, as his biographer makes him, talk so laxly as to say of a literary man, that he had no more learning than what *lie could not help.*

I remember the first introduction of Boswell on what may be called the Johnsonian stage. What is ludicrously called his *eaneigging,* began to attract notice; and my father enquired of Mr. Langton, who this novel performer was, meaning rather, I believe, to be on good

terms with him, as a frequenter in Bolt Court. The answer he received was a caution against opening his door to him. Not only were his visits described to be long, but he was known to carry, as was said perhaps by way of metaphor, his night-cap in his pocket, and to be blind to all inconvenience, and deaf to all hints, when at leisure. In rendering this account of another person, good Mr. Langton, with his usual grace of humility, and such a smile as no other countenance ever wore, would take shame to himself, and confess that he had no right to cast the first stone: and true it was; for we females of the family might get through much occupation of the after-breakfast description, drive out for two or three hours, return and dress, and my mother might turn in her mind the postponement of dinner, all within the compass of a morning-visit from Bennet Langton. But I never saw my father weary of his conversation, or knew any body complain of him as a visitor. It was with no small pride that I found the habit unimpaired when I became mistress of the house, and was myself honoured in his leisure hours, and in those of domestic affliction, with his very intimate confidence.

But to no such lengths as the undaunted James Boswell, did the superior Bennet Langton ever go. Unwilling as he always manifested himself to shift his place, the smallest perception of intrusion would have wounded him to the quick. Nay, so punctilious was he, that in visits of ceremony, he always timed himself, when returning them, by their duration and frequency when made to him. Boswell was a man of far different feeling.

My father and he, however, grew a little acquainted; and when the Life of their friend came out, Boswell showed himself very uneasy under an injury, which he was much embarrassed in defining. He called on my father, and being admitted, complained of the manner in which he was enrolled amongst Johnson's friends, which was as Mr. James Boswell of Auchinleck.

Where was the offence? It was one of those, which a complainant hardly dares

to embody in words, he would only repeat, "Well, but, *Mr. James Boswell,* surely, surely, *Mr. James Boswell."*

Gentle reader, permit me to tell thee an anecdote somewhat similar, I trust the friend who gave it me will forgive my using it. When Sir C

R — died, his family requested a friend to insert in the newspapers the article of his death, but it was to be done without eulogy or comment. The gentleman who undertook this friendly office, went himself round to the various places of reception for such information, gave the article, and paid what was demanded at each. At one, only half a crown was asked; but in the paper there published, was inserted the next morning, a request that the gentleman who had left this article at the office of the publisher, would call there at his first convenience. The request was complied with; and our friend was received by the important proprietor of the paper. The usual questions being asked, the great man proceeded to speak largely to the high character of the defunct, and to remonstrate on the brevity of the notification, but the injunction of the family was urged as a barrier to all liberty of action. Again, the virtues of Sir

C R — were recounted; and surprise was expressed that he should be thus coldly enrolled in the records of the day. No other answer could be given than that already offered. The low price paid for the insertion was then cavilled at; half a crown for inserting the death of such a man! Against this, the demand of the office was urged; but the taunt being again indecently repeated, an offer was made of any further sum that should be asked; and an open handful of mixed money being presented, the publisher took another half-crown, and bowed our friend out.

Now I conceive Mr. Boswell, in his visit to my father, to have been, equally with this man, stimulated by concern for his own interests, and nearly under the same embarrassment in conducting them. Greediness of money operated in the one case; and greediness of fame in the other. But Boswell was the more bashful of the two; he needed the assistance of the person to whom he complained, to bring the cause of his complaint to the light; and my father relieved him by guessing with some humour, that the distinction bestowed on a public singer or dancer, would have better satisfied him. "I know," said he, "Mr. Boswell, what you mean, you would have had me say that Johnson undertook this tour with The Boswell." He could not indeed absolutely covet this mode of proclamation, he would, perhaps, have been content with " the celebrated," or "the well-known," but he could not confess quite so much; he therefore acquiesced in the amendment proposed, but he was forced to depart without any promise of correction in a subsequent edition.

My father took great pains to render all his children so far independent of the opinion of the world, in the exercise of their intellects, as to remain unmolested by censure. Let it not, however, be understood that he carried this to excess in morals: on the contrary, he held in infinite contempt all affected bravery on this point; but against criticism he was proof himself, and considered this indifference as absolutely necessary to exertion. But still he would *look* at opinions; and in doing this, after Johnson's works were out of his hands, he saw, in the Gentleman's Magazine, his Life of Johnson reviewed with great asperity. Considering that the Editor was one of Johnson's most assiduous satellites, and also one of the corps who had by their representatives selected him for the office of biographer, for their own emolument, this surprised him; and calling on him, he told him that, as to the unfavourable review he had given of the work, he had his option, and he himself, as the author, should not appeal from it; but he' owned he was astonished at what he had read, as militating against an interest in which the person to whom he was speaking had a share.

The reply he received was satisfactory; it was said that the matter was not in the power of the Editor of the Gentleman's Magazine; that the review had been sent to him and in much stronger language, and that it now appeared soft-ened, as much as would be permitted. It was no part of my father's character to express gratitude for such forbearance to *himself;* but he went so far as to confess that *the work* was indebted to the Editor of the Gentleman's Magazine.

Some months after, and I can aver without any management on the subject, the late Mr. Ruggles of Spain's Hall, Essex, the author of "The Barrister," called on the Editor, purposely to ask him how he could, with any pretension to justice, admit into the Gentleman's Magazine, such a comment on a work which must be read with interest, and "for which he should be the better as long as he lived." The answer *then* given, and which I heard Mr. Ruggles repeat, was in these words, "What business had Sir J. H. to say any thing against the writings of Sterne?"

Had Sterne's writings been of a description to be put into the hands of a female, all this resentment would have belonged to *me,* because the task of reviewing, or at least of giving an opinion of them, would have been turned over to me; but, as I have said, my father had laid his affectionate injunction on me never openly or clandestinely to read what he did not approve, and had never, except *viva voce,* made me acquainted with Sterne or his writings.

And on his manner of stigmatising, I must indulge in remarking that it was never done with that common vehemence of decrying, which sometimes, in the perverseness of human nature, gives an edge to curiosity. To Sterne, as well as to other writers, he allowed all the merit he could claim, and lamented that the sad counterpoise of immorality, precluded them from general favour; and even this he did in a way that must have made any one, acting contrary to his wish, ashamed of a culpable curiosity.

For the following *jeu d?esprit,* from the lively pen of Mrs. Piozzi, I am indebted to one of those valuable friends who could, even by referring only to memory and observation, have rendered such a miscellany as this, far more worthy of attention.

Mrs. Piozzi wrote it, whilst transcrib-ing and arranging for publication, the "Letters to and from Dr. Johnson," as an anticipation of what the Monthly Review would say of what she was giving to the public. It was no premeditated effort: it was thrown on paper in the presence of a friend.

There is so much satisfaction in giving " honour to whom honour is due," that I gladly embrace this opportunity of quoting from the pen of the lady, to whom I owe the transcript of this *bijou,* the words which accompany it. "Mrs. L. who was present when Mrs. Piozzi wrote it, had long intimacy with, and a real friendship for, that eccentric, clever woman, who would have had more justice done to her talents, had she confined herself to what she really could have done, and done well, instead of attempting works for which she had not powers nor steadiness of mind."
One of Mrs. P.'s original sentiments I have it in my power to record. She said to a young friend, when speaking of cards,

"The human mind is a barrel-organ, which plays only so many tunes; and 'Cards' is one that was never pricked upon mine."

M

"The care and attention with which we have reviewed this work, was rather excited by our long expectation of it, than repaid by the instruction or amusement it affords. Let it not however be consigned to oblivion without a few remarks on its excellencies and defects, which, to say the truth, are neither of them numerous; and we should do the public double injury, in covering much paper with criticisms, upon what the Rambler himself would call *pages of inanity.* For who can it benefit, or who can it please, to hear in one letter, that poor Mrs. Salisbury had a bad night, or in another, that pretty little Sophy's head ached all yesterday.

"If the fair Editress published this correspondence to show with how much insipidity people famed for their wit and learning, might maintain a twenty years' intercourse by letter and conversation, she has succeeded admirably: but we have some little amends made us, by six more animated letters at the end, directed to Miss Boothby, whose epitaph, written by Brooke Boothby, Esq. is elegant enough. The world however is but little interested about the *slippery bowels* of a pious lady, long since dead: perhaps the strong or weakly constitutions of the living Miss Thrales, may be of more consequence to *some* men, but our reviewers are unluckily not among the number.

"We shall conclude by confessing that the correspondence bears every mark of being genuine, that Mrs. Piozzi seems confident of her success, and careless of what may be thought concerning her publication, that there are some brilliant passages, and some solid reflections, scattered up and down the book, but that, upon the whole, we find seven or eight shillings very ill bestowed on some loosely printed paper stamped with Johnson's name, which will, after all, no more render them current, than the Druid on the Paris-mine penny: it may indeed, like that penny, be laid up in some collections as curious, but never can hope to be circulated either as *useful* or *common*."

I look in vain for any thing that can connect Johnson with Sir William Jones; yet that they had come within the sphere of each other's attraction is evident, for Boswell mentions them as meeting at Mr. Beauclerk's, and it is so improbable that two such men should meet without inclination and opportunity to meet again, that I must suppose myself deficient in information. This does not however preclude me from giving what is within my reach respecting Sir W. J. himself; and in doing that, I can introduce to the reader that extraordinary personage his sister. For the former I am indebted to my younger brother. *Loquitur H. H.)* "Of Sir William Jones, the memoirs have already appeared before the public; but as what I shall say is not generally known, and is perfectly authentic, it may perhaps be acceptable. I remember to have heard him speak as a Counsel in the Court of King's Bench: the question before the Court, arose from private disagreements in a family, which made a separation

between husband and wife necessary; and there being a child whose interests were to be taken care of, the interference of the Court was required. A perfect silence prevailed — the attention of all present being attracted to hear what 'Linguist Jones,' as he was even then called, would say. Though he could not have been accustomed to hear his own voice in a court of law, for I believe this was his forensic *debut,* he, nevertheless, spoke with the utmost distinctness and clearness, not at all disconcerted by the novelty of his situation. His tone was highly declamatory, accompanied with what Pope has called 'balancing his hands,' and he seemed to consider himself as much a public orator as Cicero or Hortensius could have done. His oration, for such it must be called, lasted, I recollect, near an hour. But the orator, however he might wish to give a grand idea of the office of a pleader, did not, in the course of the business, entirely avoid the ridiculous; for having occasion to mention a case decided by the Court, he stated in the same high declamatory tone in which he had delivered the whole of his speech, that he found 'that it had been argued *by one Mr. Baldwin.'* Not being very conversant with the state of the bar, he did not know that this *one Mr. Baldwin* was, at the time of which I am speaking, a barrister in great business, and was then sitting not half a yard from the orator's elbow. It occasioned a smile, or perhaps more than a smile, on every countenance in Court; but the orator proceeded as steadily as before. In the course of his speech, he had had occasion to mention the governess of the child; and he had done it in such terms as conveyed, and must have conveyed to any one possessed of ordinary powers of comprehension, an idea that she was an extremely improper person to remain with a young lady: on the next day, therefore, Mr. Jones appeared again in the seat which he had occupied the preceding day; and when the judges had taken their seats, he began with the same high declamatory tone, to inform the Court, that "it was with *the deepest regret* he had learned that, in what he

had had the honour to state to their Lordships the preceding day, he was understood to mean to say that Mrs. was a harlot!!" The gravity of every countenance in Court yielded to the attack thus made upon it, and a general laugh was produced by it."

With the sister of Sir "William Jones I was personally acquainted. She was the frequent visitor of Lady Prime, and attached herself veryclosely to our friend Mrs. Welch. My mother, with whom Mrs. W. was not by many degrees so great a favourite as with my father, used to consider these two lady geniuses as excellently coupled; but I do not think Mrs. Welch took to Miss Jones as cordially as she would have done to a less eccentric character. It is a precipitate judgment which leads us into the supposition that similarity produces cohesion. Mrs. Welch often smiled at the departures from common usage, observable in Miss Jones, and latterly found them intrusive. Severe she could not be; and to the sisterly exertions of Miss Jones she did high honour, fully sensible how much the world was obliged to them; but there were female friends of much lower claims, in whose company she seemed to take more pleasure, though, perhaps, in all her acquaintance, there was no other on whom her extent of knowledge would not in some points have been thrown away. With regard to my own standing with her, her affection was habit: she never demanded any thing of me; but if I showed any wish for knowledge she would encourage me. I had not even a right to be jealous:—but we were surprised that Miss Jones did not produce "more sensation." Lady H. was duly sensible to the sterling worth of Mrs. Welch; but, early in their acquaintance, an unfortunate circumstance had placed her on a very *ow fourm* in my mother's opinion. Lady H. was working a large carpet, when Mr. Welch and his daughters came to spend some time at Twickenham. The young ladies assiduously offered their services, and professed a feeling of pride in being allowed to contribute to such a great performance; but never never could my mother forget that her first business after they were gone, was to undo what they had done. The *esprit de Vaiguille* is a very lively feeling amongst *us,* and proficiency in the art is often made a test of worth, by those who perhaps would not like to be excelled.—I question whether Lady H. 's opinion of Mrs. Clive, as an actress, was not lowered by her putting tulips of an unnatural colour into the carpet which she worked for Horace Walpole.

The mother and sister of Sir William Jones resided at Oxford, where the former died at a great age; they had devoted themselves to the interests of their extraordinary relative, and to such intensity did they carry their affectionate assiduities, that to save his expenses, when expense was not convenient, the work of a tailor was done by their hands.

Miss Jones was of no very sightly appearance; and her negligence of dress could hardly be carried lower; she was said to have pursued a track of learning similar to that which distinguished her brother, but this I had no means of ascertaining; and she was one of a small number of persons, whose conversation seems to be made purposely trifling, as if to veil their own superiority. There are some still living, who, even now, when society is so much more on an intellectual equality than formerly, practise this. It is a very bad plan of being agreeable, and really often calls in question the veracity of those who have endeavoured to give a favourable impression of others. Miss Jones would walk through London, and four miles out of it, with a Greek folio under her arm; but I remember hearing her, on the mention of the Merchant of Venice in a house of little literature, ask if there was not a pretty song in it about Jessica; and in a morning visit I have known her affect the French style of light conversation, till she was more wearying than any prosing repeater of circumstantials.

She had some paradoxes in her opinions, and was not withheld from argument even by the knowledge that she was arguing absurdly. She would contend, that nobody could sleep the worse for drinking green tea, though she

owned her brother drank it at the expense of his night's rest.

Her residences were various, but distance was no impediment to her; nor did she regard weather or consult health. She would wade through dirt, so ill provided against it, that whatever wet mud she had not left on the stairs or the carpet, she would wring out of the feet of her stockings and the hems of her petticoats, into the hearth; a It is very probable that many will join her in her opinion of the impunity with which this delicious beverage may be indulged in; and without question, its action is very various. But one instance of what it *can* do was afforded by the late Dr. Shaw, of the Museum, who, solely for the sake of experiment, practised drinking it till he had lost the use of one arm. This I heard from himself, and he concluded the recital very gravely, by saying, " And then, Madam, when I had carried the experiment thus far, I discontinued it, and recovered the use of my arm." bright steel fender was no impediment. All this Mrs. Welch would take in perfect good humour, adding to it the amusement of a housemaid's despair, when called to assist thus in increasing her own labour. But no. such departures from decorum were observable in her own conduct. On the contrary, there was a respect for "property" in her mind, and she entered the " apartments" of her friends, as she would have done those of the palaces of Rome, Naples, or Genoa. The reader will bear with me while I indulge in the recollection of her farewell words in her last *sejour* with us. "I have to thank you for more pleasure than at my time of life I thought myself capable of feeling."

There was one old friendship, old I suppose it was, because I know no other cement for it but age, on which Miss Jones set a high value; this was with a military veteran, a General Martin, but who was known in ladies' card-parties, by the distinguishing prefix of Cupid. I believe he was of a very great age, but he kept himself in excellent repair. No lady ever could boast a finer complexion; his dress was of the same delicacy, and *f* his manners those of what

is called, without, I presume, meaning any thing antediluvian, "the first world. " I remember once being his partner at a whist-table, when some mistake was committed, which a gentleman on the other side followed with words not quite *en regie.* The General was not at all jsoved, but he was firm; one *must* give way; the offender came to his recollection, and apologised. In quitting the table, the General said to me with all possible gravity of speech, and erection of his not very tall person, "I am glad, Ma'am, the gentleman apologised, otherwise I must have *noticed* it." The idea, serious in itself, and in its possible consequences, was rendered so very ludicrous by the accompaniments, that it required a little command of countenance to receive it as it was given.

We lost sight of Miss Jones, by her going for a time to Bristol or its neighbourhood, whence she returned under the style and title of matrimony; but of the circumstances of this change, and of him who occasioned it, I know nothing. I think I remember to have heard that she became a widow, but she appeared to hold to her friends by so slender a thread, that its giving way was hardly perceived. informed mind could follow him, and with an accuracy and precision of judgment, so satisfactory, as to induce the parties in the cause, when apprised of the issue of their lawsuit, to instruct their counsel to make their acknowledgments to the court, as having been the means of restoring peace and harmony to private families, and having done every thing that the parties desired. He was not what was considered a *profound lawyer,* when the term is applied to *technical* niceties in pleading, nor did he seem to have any very elevated opinion of that species of knowledge, or of those who possessed it. Mr. Wallace, who had been Attorney General, and who was deeply versed in that department of legal information, and Mr. Howarth, who, however honourable and praiseworthy his conduct might be, was infinitely inferior to Wallace, happened to die at the same time. When Lord Mansfield was told of their death, he scarcely expressed any concern for Mr.

Wallace, but very great regret for Mr. Howarth.

When my brother Henry gave me an anecdote connecting the names of Lord Mansfield and Johnson, I asked him for any little memoir of the former that might be in his recollection; I am therefore obliged to him for the following, which I wish I had introduced less awkwardly.

"Of Lord Mansfield's intellectual powers, his great comprehension, or his eloquence, it is needless to say a word, as the Concurrent testimony of all who could form a judgment of him, has already placed him among the first men of his time; but of the wise and honourable use of those talents, it may be permitted to one who perfectly well remembers him, though but in his latter days, to mention that of which he was an ear-witness. Many a time I have heard him deliver the decision of the court on abstruse points of law, with a profundity of reasoning, where scarcely even a well

"His disregard of the lawyers of the description above mentioned, led him to treat lightly those legal ceremonies which were connected with such attainments. At the making of a Serjeant he has been known to laugh so heartily, that he was scarcely able to do that which his office required him to do.

"In addition to this instance of Lord Mansfield's light estimation of those who were considered by such as could best judge, as the most skilful, we might subjoin his treatment of Mr. Serjeant Hill, whose name has already been mentioned in this work. I have seen the Serjeant standing up in the court, immovable as a statue, and looking at no object, and arguing in support of his client's cause, so wrapt up in the workings of his own mind, as, seemingly at least, to be insensible to any objects around him. In the midst of his argument, which was frequently so perplexed by parenthesis within parenthesis, as to excite the laughter of the whole Court, Lord Mansfield would interrupt him with, Mr. Serjeant, Mr. Serjeant;' he was rather deaf, — the words were repeated without effect; at length, the

counsel sitting near him would tell him that his Lordship spoke to him: this roused him: Lord M. would then address him with, The Court hopes your cold is better.' All this was done with a tone, and in a manner which showed that he wished to make the object of this apparent civility in fact an object of ridicule; and so far it must be considered as having succeeded; how far it was perfectly decorous in a judge, sitting in his Court, to indulge this little love of mischief, for we do not wish to call it by a harsh name, others may decide; but certainly he was very agreeable to the bar in other respects; indeed, whenever this foible did not show itself, his patient attention, his *assisting* questions, if I may be allowed the term, and his intuitive comprehension of what was submitted to his understanding, made him an exceedingly pleasant judge to those who were called to argue deep questions before him.

"Of his eloquence in either the House of Lord9 or of Commons, I cannot say any thing; but of his speeches in the Court of King's Bench, I can say that they were always pertinent, with respect to the subject before him; nothing was said for effect, nothing theatrical. It is known, that, when in the House of Commons, he was considered as the antagonist to Mr. Pitt; and the writers of that period of our history inform us, that on very many occasions he showed himself Pitt's superior, and plucked the laurel from his brows, on questions, where, perhaps, the popular feeling was in Pitt's favour, which is very credible if his judges were cool and dispassionate, as Pitt's speeches depended much on his tone and manner to produce the desired effect; without which many of them would be considered as having but slender claims to attention." / have nothing to say to Lord Mansfield's abilities. The now well-known story of *Elm wet,* and *Elm dry,* shows the readiness of his wit to extricate him from a pinching dilemma.

The following is, perhaps, not so public. His Lordship, it is well known, had too much of the spirit of John Knox, or something equally unfettering, to pay

any great regard to the holidays appointed by the Church of England. He had not suspended the business of the court in which he presided, for the sake of Ash Wednesday and even this decision of "currat lex" had given offence to some who regarded the commencement of Lent; but making an attempt to proceed with business on Good Friday, he was resisted by Serjeant Davy, who, on his announcing his intention, told him that his Lordship would be "the first judge that had done so since Pontius Pilate."

As connected with Johnson in a pursuit, but I do not think I can say on the footing of his conversation-friends, I must again, and may now more particularly present to the reader's notice, that anomaly in society, George Steevens. He had introduced himself to my father by letter, before the year 1770, and while we were at Twickenham; and I can remember, when waiting for orders and directions by the side of my father's table, being very much struck with the delicate penmanship of these epistles. On my observing it, Sir. J. told me that they were most troublesome applications from a man of whom he knew but little, but who was soliciting him, notwithstanding his being employed on the History of Music, to read Shakspeare anew, and furnish him with fresh remarks. The answers to these repeated requests, would, I can pretty well guess, have silenced any one but the person to whom they were addressed.

My mother's health was never so good in the country as in town, or at least her dislike to the country injured it; and this combining with my lather's wish to have my brothers near him, made him quit Twickenham, and reside wholly in London. Steevensthen changed his mode of attack—he presented himself in person, and succeeded so far as to get my father to recollect, and consider and discuss with him, passages in the plays that admitted of elucidation.

Steevens had too much power of rendering himself agreeable, to be felt as an intruder, where he was not thoroughly known. Beside this, he could make his services valuable, and there are, in the last volume of the History of Music, some proofs of his prompt genius, for which the compiler of such a work could not but feel very much obliged.

He was now in the most sociable intercourse at our house. He would be with us by nine in the morning; but nothing would induce him to share our breakfast, or to mend his own, though he had walked from Hampstead.

At his villa there, which had been the wellknown house of entertainment, dear to the *devotes* of Richardson's "Clarissa," we often visited him in a morning drive. He valued himself as possessing in his lawn, the only piece of level ground of the same size in Hampstead; but of his desert of this privilege, he gave a very indifferent proof, when he boasted of his sagacity in getting rid of an inconvenience attached to it. It had a spring of good water and a pump, from which the inhabitants, when it was a public house, used to supply themselves. This was certainly intolerable to — I may say such a coxcomb: — a foot set on his *foot,* he would probably have better endured, than if set on his lawn; but, surely, situated as the spring was, he might have accommodated the matter, without being unneighbourly; — but no — he chuckled at the device he had adopted of changing the hour of drawing water so often, as to weary the patience of those who needed it, and oblige them to go further.

The house was of the true cockney description, — by the road-side, but disguising this by an entrance through the garden; — plate glass windows raised it to a character of elegance — the library was a lady's *boudoir;* and it was at this time furnishing, as if for the reception of a bride. To this probability Lady H. alluded, on his exhibiting the apartments, by saying, "You want nothing now but a wife." His answer was in these words: "*That,* as well as the rest of my furniture, is bespoke."

Not a word of truth was there in the assertion— the nearest approach, I believe, which he ever made to the possessing *such* a piece of furniture, was borrowing or usurping from a friend;

for it was, I fear, too well proved, that the domestic peace of a family had suffered severely under his cool profligacy. He was not a man, I am confident, who had to plead the impetuosity of passion, which in the moral of the world is ranked as a grace, if not as a virtue. He was a frigid calculator, a sort of bystander to his own actions; and in his neighbourhood, as his true character unfolded itself, his attentions to young women were considered not as in themselves seductive, but as a blasting mildew which would injure their estimation. I know, in particular, one young person who was cautioned against receiving even what may be called *literary* favours, lest her being seen speaking to him, might mark her as to be shunned by others.

My brothers were school-boys—I was my father's *fag in ordinary,* and passed without notice; but on my younger brother, who had a taste for poetry, he bestowed great attention, and assisted very much in its improvement. He set him exercises that required intellectual exertion, and tried his patience and perseverance by little variations in his demands, without the novelty of a fresh subject; but he was not niggardly in encouragement. Two and sixpence for turning Gay's melodious "Go Rose" into Latin verse, was munificence to one who delighted in the labour; and Mr. Steevens's coming was hailed as the renewal of pleasure.

But can it be credited that a mind so fraught as was that of this elegant scholar, with classic recollections,—that a man of such incessant industry and occupation, and who seemed to have no moments for thought that did not forward his great undertaking, should be guilty of all the petty faults of the scandal-mongers of a village, and the gossips of a card-table. Yet so it was; and he would talk of the interior of families and the trifles of ceconomy, till his conversation was disgusting and contemptible. With the most manly sense of the sublime and beautiful—enraptured when repeating passages from the finest poets—regardless of all personal inconvenience, and superior to all the com-

mon modes of passing time, he yet could panegyrize the delicacy of furniture, make nonsense of indispensable importance, and affect to be a follower of fashionable folly. It grieved him, that we in London had a white dog; he spoke with abhorrence of any thing that might soil his carpets, or tread down the grass on his lawn; and of his affectation, I can give an incredible proof.

He had strolled in to sit with my father one very warm evening in July. We were still in town, and at the close of a day of fatiguing heat, such a visitor was orgeat and lemonade. He sat till near ten, and then said he wished he had a chance of spending the next hours as agreeably as the two last. This naturally exciting a question, he said that he was engaged to a masquerade, his man was waiting with his dress; and then he began one of his descants on the horror of coming out into daylight in the morning, in a hat and feathers, a domino— and, to use his own phrase, "one's white satin shoes." All this was nonsensical; he was certainly not bound to be ridiculous, even in his *own* eyes.

But there was no danger; he was under no such obligation or engagement; no whiter shoes was he called on to wear, than those made white by the dust of the Hampstead Road, for he was going straight home, and thither he went; there he staid, and employed himself in his usual way, rising with the lark the next morning.

Till the character of Steevens was entirely ruined by his own imprudence, the acquaintance with him went on with tolerable smoothness, but with nothing that merited the name of confidence. My father could not relish his worrying Garrick, though he himself thought as contemptuously as any one could do of the Stratford jubilee. To Steevens it was still, even in recollection, high merriment; he had written innumerable squibs in the St. James's Chronicle, in which he had a share, and, having cut them out as they appeared, he gave them to my brother as *morceaux d'esprit.* Nine-tenths of them were as flat as possible; they had no characteristic but that of teasing irritating malice towards a man, the most valuable part of whose library was then in loan to him for the improvement of his own work.

One very pretty thing he wrote, for the purpose, as he said in his own phrase, " of keeping up the ball;" that is to say, keeping public attention alive while the Shakspeare was printing. This was a ballad entitled " Shakspeare's Bed-side," representing the poet as sick, and sending for various doctors. The commentators were then described as proposing remedies and trying experiments; there was wit and humour, and no malice in this.

But there was a sad suspicion excited in my father's breast, which, while there was any preservation of character on the part of Steevens, he kept there, strong as circumstances were against him. The American war had involved the country in a situation which made it the duty of all who wished to see it safe out of it, to offer every means of assistance in their power; and the magistrates of the county thought proper to address the

N throne with patriotic offers of their services. My father was to draw up the address; it was done, I had copied it for the previous perusal of the secretary of stats, and had laid it down on a corner of the library-table, when Mr. Steevens came in, at an hour not usual. He made his visit.

To send away the address was perhaps the next concern; it was gone, and I had to copy it again.

This would have been trifling, but the next morning it appeared in the St. James's Chronicle, of which, I have already hinted, the editor of Shakspeare was a proprietor!

I cannot make the public pay for repetitions to which I am conscious. In the former volume, I have stated the ill offices of Mr. Steevens to effect a coolness between Mr. Garrick and my father, and have detailed the concluding circumstances of Sir J. H.'s turning him. out of the house by his collar; therefore I will in this place only bring to recollection the fact.

It must not be supposed that this indignity with which Sir J. H. had treated this wrong-headed man, was taken quite

passively. The St. James's Chronicle was still at hand, and in it soon appeared the effusions of his wrath. My father was abused in excellent poetry; his Jove for music was introduced, by saying, that its sounds

"Play round the head, but never reach his heart:"

And his pride was described in the assertion, that he "Scarce deign'd to kneel when knighted by the crown."

It would be unfair to deny the wit and brilliancy of this invective. My father gave it its due praise, but the advantage at which he had his libeller was quite sufficient to satisfy, without departing from justice.

In addition to the atrocious conduct of Steevens with regard to a friend's conjugal peace, there stood out against him an accusation of great want of ready courage in himself, when in the Essex militia, on some occasion when courage was in request. The two circumstances seemed to unite for the purpose to which it was then useful to put them, and my father wrote and sent to the St. James's Chronicle an epigram, which has been confessed, by good judges, one of the best in our language, whether the pertinence, the terseness, or the point be considered. It was this; —

"The dark designing villain's art,
His teeming brain, his ranc'rous heart,
Great Shakspeare to unfold,
Iago's horrid portrait draws,
In breach of friendship's sacred laws,
And fiend-like malice bold.

"His muse, assuming humour's guise,
Laughs at Parolles, and blinds his eyes
While he betrays his lord;
A liar, coward, braggart vain,
The soldier's scorn, of arms the stain,
    A scoundrel on record!

"Our Editob the poet's page
Illustrates, and to teach the age
A truth but little known,
That two such characters may meet,
And in one bosom fix their seat,
    Unites tbem in his own."

The shop of Payne, the bookseller, at the Mews Gate, was at this time the resort of the London *literati*. This place was as little calculated as any could well be, for the reception of the number who

not only *frequented* it, but during certain hours of the day, were never out of it. It was, as is well known, though probably the traces of it may soon be gone, at the gate of the lower Mews, opening into Castle Street, Leicester Fields; an elbow-shed, rather than shop, and lighted by a skylight. Crossing obliquely the gate of the Mews, Payne had a good dwelling-house, the ground-floor windows of which, as seen from the street, were fairly barricaded with books. *H. H.* says further.) In this *nookery* were to be found, about one every day, such men as the Rev. Mr. Cracherode, Mr. Southwell, Mr. Tyrrwhitt, the Bishop of Dromore (at that time, Dr. Percy), Dr. Heberden, Bennet Langton, George Steevens, Sir J. H., and others. Mr. Cracherode, Mr. Tyrrwhitt, and Mr. Southwell, were as regular as the day itself, much to the annoyance of Payne, who found them very much in his way; the rest were occasionally, but very generally, to be seen there. With a hope of attracting some of these literary loungers,

Henry Payne, a younger brother of Johnson's publisher, opened a very handsome shop, almost opposite Marlborough

House, in Pall Mall, but the business was not brisk. The

Mr. Tyrrwhitt was the learned editor of Chaucer, a book beyond all praise, and such as, for the information and erudition contained in it, scarcely any man but himself could have given to the world; he was one of the first who decided that the Poems obtruded on the public as Rowley's, were forgeries. As these Poems are now mentioned, I will just add, that when I asked Dr. Johnson his opinion of them, he expressed his conviction fl.at they were not genuine, but his as certain conviction that they were not Chatterton's, and that if Chatterton had any hand in them *at all,* he must have had very great assistance.

Dr. Percy had edited the Reliques of Ancient Poetry, a man with great conversation-talents, owner used to remark on the vexatious power *of* habit, which made these gentlemen, so desirable as visitors to *him,* prefer his namesake's dark dirty encumbered shop, to his which was certainly in all points very attractive. My father did all he could for H. P., who had a large family. He employefl one of his sons to catalogue his library, and, I may mention as matter of curiosity, that the rough draught being completed, it was laid aside in the shop to be fair copied, but inadvertently it was moved one evening, so as that the centre of the manuscript came on the cork of a bottle newly filled with spirit of salt! I need not say that the work was to be in great measure done again.

but I am not prepared to say that he was a deep scholar. It is well known that he was the author of the elegant popular song,

"Oh! Nanny, wilt thou go with me?"

Of Bennet Langton, I shall here mention only the names of some of those men of letters, who formed the society of his house, such as the Wartons, Mr. Windham, Dr. Charles Burney, Lord Monboddo, Taylor (then called " the gigantic philosopher," now known as the profound Platonist), and Porson. Of the last, I can truly say, that no man could communicate knowledge with less ostentation: what he said was spoken as if it had been what any one might have known, even when discussing that which called for the recollection of what commentators had said on it. Pages of Junius he had by heart; but these have been learned by others. Any advantage that Eentley had over Porson, probably was confined to Oriental learning. It is to the honour of Reimar's edition of Dion Cassius, that Porson thought it one of the best edited works he knew.

Recollections of the tenderest kind are called up by the mention of this exquisite ballad, which I have been told was Dr. Percy's invitation to his charming wife, on her release from her twelvemonths' confinement in the royal nursery, in attendance on her charge, Prince Edward, the late Duke of Kent. His Royal Highness's temper as a private gentleman did not discredit his nurse; for his humanity was conspicuous. The best whole length of the so often painted wife of Rubens will always keep in remembrance what Mrs. Percy was, par-

ticularly that in the engravings from the Luxembourg gallery, where " Lady Rubens" appears under the character of Mary de Medicis kneeling to receive the crown.

I wish some person of sufficient information could tell me that I err, in thinking that the air of " Oh! Nanny," applauded and doated on as it is, has not obtained that celebrity for its author that he merits. I suppose it the composition of Carter,—but who knows Carter? and what can better make a man known than such a production?

Mr. Cracherode was a man of great literary intelligence; I do not know that he was particularly eminent as a classical scholar, but a very good medalist, and might, had it not been for a certain melancholy shyness, which appeared in his manners, his habits, and conversation, have been a most valuable acquisition in society.

So just was my father's quarrel against Steevens considered, that from the time of his breaking with him, no one of the frequenters of the Mews Gate would ever hold any communication with him,, excepting Mr. Cracherode, who himself a lowspirited shy man, perhaps did not feel equal to the avowal of indignation even by silence.

Circumstances occurring at Hampstead, likewise, contributed to degrade this strange incongruous slave of malevolent caprice. His closing years were marked still more deeply by increasing and unaccountable habits of seclusion; and he whose mirth and talents I have heard admitted in excuse of servants inattentive at tables where he dined, became worse than lost to those who had most valued him. His end was said to have been such as would not bear description, — little short of that of Voltaire.

But in abhorrence as I hold the moral turpitude of Steevens, I cannot recollect without a mixt feeling of interest and regret, the hours in which I have listened to his conversation. Such con *Listened,* I may truly say, of *my* share in this, and the other colloquial pleasures of that period; for no other paryersation could not be heard without interest, and much do I

now regret that I did not then commit to paper some of its leading features. The motto of this volume, and one anecdote, are all I can now redeem; the latter is this, and for its truth I can refer only to Steevens himself; a sorry reference, I confess.

He said that he was in the pit at the Opera, when he saw a gentleman come in, and seat himself with great composure, notwithstanding the ticipation in them can I boast. It may be supposed that I was brought forward in the society that I describe, and I may be envied for distinction, or aspersed as of that odious set denominated the *bat bleu,* by which I understand female gladiators, instigated by a contemptible vanity; for to no rational and useful members of society would I apply it. 1, therefore, wish to present myself to the reader's imagination, as I stood in general by a window, having fastened to whatever I could find adaptable to my purpose, one end of an almost interminable piece of netting, then required for an addition to our dress, or at other times employed in needlework, always silent, except when called upon by my father to take directions, or sent on some mission to his books. Nay, sometimes I was to be found kneeling at a window-seat, that I might proceed with my task of copying, independent of interruptions; thus I remember I was disposed of, when my father *ejected* Mr. Steevens. My eldest brother gave me the jocose name of " the camel," from the frequency of this posture.

incongruities of his dress drew upon him the eyes of all near enough to observe him. His hair was in the highest style of the evening fashion: his coat and waistcoat were fit for court; but the lower part of his habiliments was adapted to horse-exercise. When most likely to be gazed on, he took from his pocket a large clasp-knife: he opened it, wiped the blade on his knee, as any wood-cutter might have done, and then pulling out from another pocket a large piece of bread and another of cheese, he cut and ate them with the most immovable gravity.

Mr. S. said he could only conclude

that it was done for a wager: it is this moderation of opinion that inclines me to give credit to the story; had it been a fiction, I think he would have gone on to explain it.

When I began to put together this undigested work, 1 was prohibited from making it a tax, even on my recollection: I therefore put aside every thing that detained my mind. The prohibition is now removed, and under the consequent license I may, however cautious, have wearied the reader by mistaking what is interesting only to myself, for that which is of general interest. This I hazard, under the probability that the number of those who can never be told too much, may be as great

'as that of those who say, who cares for this?

Perhaps, I have as little cause to fear on the subject which calls out my apology, as on any I can present. I have said in my former volume, less than I might have done of the well known Bennet Langton. It will be relief to my mind to turn from my last memoir to him.

Mr. Langton was formed for contemplation and the intercourse of the tongue; and those who knew him in his family, or amongst his literary friends, might, without injustice, have characterised him as uAerly unfit for every species of activity; inactive, I believe he was by nature, to the last ; degree of what is not *very* wonderful , but here I will refer those who wish to know what is a *ponderful* degree of activity, to the Suffolk or Essex story. Pray do not let me slander a county. Two gentlemen were riding through a field, in which, under a tree, lay three what are called " hulking fellows." "I wonder which is the laziest of those men," said Mr. A. "We will try," said Mr. B. "You fellows there!

he affords one of the many lessons to be extracted from the practice of the conscientious; for I have been told, that when encamped on Warley Common, with the Lincoln militia, there was not a better or a more efficient officer. Here I presume the imperious call of duty was obeyed without any reference to habit; and in another part of his character this

was conspicuous; for I have heard him say that indulgence in wine was, in him, a natural inclination, and that the need he felt of it to reinforce his powers, was painful; but the idea of Bennet Langton what is called "overtaken," is too preposterous to be dwelt on.

He at one time had a view to accepting some part in the education of the princes; but he was not aware of the exhaustion of such an employment, or he would have declined it; his great height and comparative slenderness, gave no idea of strength adequate to any thing more than his modes of life required. I have heard him say, when sitting in conversation with only myself, that about two o'clock in the day he felt such a failure of his powers, as entirely to disperse all his ideas; he said he grew forgetful and confused, but was presently himself again, on taking a little food.
here's an apple for you ; come, fetch it." "Bring it yourself," cried the first speaker. Mr, B. approached, but would not give it to the man who had answered him; he offered it to the second, who bade him put it into his mouth. He turned to the third, who made it a condition of his acceptance, that he should "wag his jaws" for him. The counties must have improved since this libel was invented.
What nourishment he might take in his family, I know not, but from a dinner-party, he might have risen fasting, and unconscious *of* it, such was the perpetual flow of his conversation, and so incessant were the claims made on him.

I need not say that his connections and associations were of the best class. He might have made his house one of the first "*esprit shops,*" as I have heard the rallying points of conversationsociety humorously called: but all pretension was foregone by the quietness of his character, and Lady Rothes's cordial domestic manners would have put all affectation to the blush. She loved all her friends too sincerely to admit of any *minauderie,* and those who had put on any occasional *graces,* would soon have found that, in proportion as they departed from what was perfectly natural, they missed in their endeavour to recom-

mend themselves.

It was his intention to educate his children at home, and under only parental tutelage. He, therefore, after some removes from his first abode, settled in Westminster, determined to live very quietly, and devote himself to this grand duty, in which the children of both sexes were to be equally considered; he told my father he should not only give his sons, but his daughters, a knowledge of the learned languages, and that he meant to familiarise the latter to the Greek language to such perfection, that while five of his girls employed themselves in feminine works, the sixth should read a Greek author for the general amusement.

The scheme was arranged, and every thing was to give way to it. Society was to be curtailed down to friendships; a curtailment which, in some houses, might produce all the quiet and leisure that could be wished, but which had little visible effect in this; nothing was to be done in vain, and all the allurements of the metropolis were to be set at nought. That any which were indecorous or even idle, would be confidently defied, all who knew Bennet Langton might safely pledge their faith; but that he could withstand the elegant seductions of polished society, and the charms of lettered conversation, was not so certain.

To Lady Rothes, who had no wish but to do the best that could be done for this numerous family,—who, with all her natural easy dignity, had not an atom of pride or egotism, nothing was a difficulty that demanded only sacrifices from herself. There was no fear of the want of subjects of the highest interest to *her,* for every place would afford her the satisfaction of comforting the unhappy, and supplying the needy; and Westminster was as fruitful in this species of harvest as any one could wish. The family character for extensive benevolence was soon published, and a basket found at the house-door one morning early, made all the little ladies happy and industrious, when it turned out a small being, which cried for food, and required change of raiment. I do not think the fortunate *expose* was ever claimed. I am sure it was never deserted. Mr. Langton's prompt benevolence once placed him in a most amiable point of view, and flattered me with the hope of an interesting occupation. He had called on my father, who happened to be out. The carriage was at the door, he therefore made no farther enquiry, but left his ticket, and departed. Presently he returned, leading in a very pretty little girl, without any walking habiliments, who was able just to speak so as to be perfectly unintelligible to strangers; he had found her astray near the door, a man had taken hold on her, but could do nothing towards restoring her to her home. i, girl-like, was delighted with this "treasure trove;" it had long been the avowed wish of my heart that some one would leave an infant at the door, and now my wish seemed fulfilled. I stript little missy, but no clue was to be found, and now my mind expatiated in the delight of taking this charge on myself; I had settled every thing but.her fortune and her wedding-clothes in a few minutes. Mr. Langton and my mother,' however, being rather more cool-headed, it was proposed that we should drive to every place that we could at all conjecture the child meant to name; we did so, but still all was fruitless endeavour. We set Mr. Langton down at his own house, and returned to ours by a new *route*. Still I was safe in my guardianship, but at our door were waiting two females of very respectable appearance, who, in the greatest agitation, claimed my ward, and were recognised by her. The child had wandered after a servant, allured by the hope of an apple, and the man who had found her, had inadvertently led her *from* her home.

St. James's Park was at hand. Mr. Langton's friends preached at the Chapel Royal, agreeable conversationists were met in great frequency. Mr. Langton walked and talked; he was attracted to hear the sermons of those whom he knew and valued; little *soirees* were formed; unceremonious 'dinners followed; it was of absolute necessity that he should appear at the levee; his

lady was looked for at the drawing-rooms; and, in short, Mr. Langton found, though perhaps he would have been the last to take a compliment to himself, that however firmly he might resolve, a man so agreeable and accessible, could not in London, or in any situation affording society of a high class, live out of request. I fear that in speaking of Boswell I may have referred *to* a fact not yet introduced; but I cannot, without more than adequate exertion, ascertain this. Had I foreseen the trouble which I undertook in collecting for these volumes, which may after all appear very negligently arranged, I should have avoided it; but I am too far gone for repentance. I allude to Boswell's story of a lady "who requested a guest at her table not to cut a mango, because it had cost two shillings, and who, at the same time, was ruining her husband by her expenses."

Nothing of this having a shadow of truth in it but the presence of the mango, Lady Rothes, who knew the slander to

"Iii vain were the attempts at a home-education. Mr. Langton knew not how much the possession of extensive learning sometimes overshoots the power of communicating first elements; he was bewildered in his own labyrinth of ideas, and I believe, was a little sickened of his plan, by the late king's frequently repeated enquiry, " How does education go on?" and by the subsequent advice, to remember that

"A little learning is a dangerous thing."

I have now and then, to my cost, had occasion to know that it is dangerous to write what would be well received if spoken. So much depends on countenance, tone, and manner, none of which can be conveyed on paper, that it is prudent to check all those little sallies, which in a mirthful moment may suggest themselves to us while writing, if they can by any construction be tortured into offence.

be aimed at herself, asked Boswell how he could put together such a falsity. He replied, affecting the tone of Johnson, "Why, Madam, it is no more than is done sby landscapepainters; the land-

scape is from nature, and they put a tree in the foreground as an embellishment." Was this man a safe member of society? I once said in a letter, when meaning that I was going to be very busy, that "I should drive the world before me," and it was quoted against me, years after, as a proof of my haughtiness! So let the merry be cautious. But there is much more effect produced even in speaking, where an elevated situation makes favour or displeasure matter almost of life or death. Mr. Langton, who would with inimitable humour tell stories reflecting on his height, could not well digest his Majesty's caution, or his saying to him at a review at Ashford, " So, I suppose you have been staying with Lord L; he has got a sweet dirty hole in this country; but it is a comfort that if you had sunk into the mud, your long legs would have helped you out again. " To the *voit* that he excited, Mr. Langton ever did justice: he did so fully, in the following instance. A new fashion of a loose wrapping-coat had been introduced in a very severe winter, and every wall, and the front of every empty house were placarded with the bills of rival tailors, setting forth their great choice of these great coats and their prices: gentlemen, be their height or size what it might, were to be fitted in a moment.

Mr. Langton went to one of these repositories, and found waiting in the shop a very short thick man, whom it appeared not easy to suit. Not less difficult was it to find a coat long enough for Mr. Langton. No coat was to be found to fit either. The first comer began to murmur, and Mr. Langton followed him in complaining of this disappointment, and reminding the man of his undertaking, he replied, "Gentlemen, I do indeed undertake to furnish great coats for persons of all sizes; but I do not make them for hop *sacks* or for hop *poles.*"

On a very different occasion, his slenderness called out the wit of a man, when in some popular meeting he had occasion to address the people assembled. "Don't mind what that fellow says," cried out this Merry Andrew of the mob; "you see he only wants a place in the Victualling Office."

His sons, who have a similar advantage over the heads of their neighbours, have more witty things to tell, but it is not my province to speak of *them;* they amused the good people of Paris, by raising their arms to let them pass. But, if I am correct in my observation, they are not by many degrees so pre-eminent as their height would have rendered them half a century ago. The race of our countrymen is, probably, improved by the superior good sense with which they are reared. Whoever recollects the Parade at St. James's in the time of the American war, when the officers in the guards were drest with curls, loaded with Marechalle powder, long hair plaited, delicate white gaiters, &c. and scented cambric handkerchiefs, when the first lines of a song,

"Teddy, my godson, an officer bold,
Just turn'd of a dozen and one,"
were rather descriptive than libellous, and young men of, fashion called it *service* to take a sedan chair to mount Opera-guard, must with pleasure
. contemplate the change which the exigencies of war, and I may, I believe, add the ferocity of the modern Hannibal, have effected. We may abuse and vilify, and caricature those who have obeyed these calls on their vigilance, so we may paint ass's ears and a tail to the sun, but he shines on, and sadly should we miss him if he failed us.
We pay our country a compliment in passing unnoticed things similar to some which are handed down to us, as re

My brother Henry always described as a choice treat, the good fortune of finding Mr. Langton at home in a forenoon, with only those about him whose part it was to be attentive. His mind would then expand into the most diffusive recollections; and his ideas would, as indeed was often the case, flow too fast to get out of the way of each other. But on such occasions little heed was taken of the fire. He would, perhaps, pause to say that it would go out, if not attended to, but this was a brief and disregarded interruption. He would resume the thread of his discourse, but presently awakened by the

sense of impending inconvenience, he would proceed so far as to say, "Pray ring for coals," but no one yet stirred. Then he would get into the most fluent recitation of half a page of Greek, breaking off for fear of wearying, by saying, as I well remember was his phrase, "and so it goes on," accompanying his words with a gentle wave of his hand, indicating that you might better suppose the rest than bear his proceeding. But still the fire was going more nearly out. He would then a little alter his tone, and say intreatingly, "*Do,* pray, ring for coals." All quiet, perhaps indeed *looking* at the fire, he would launch out into the most delightfully apt quotation from Hudibras, or, as /have heard him, into Anstey's Pleader's Guide. "Did any body answer the bell?" he would ask. "No, Sir." Did any body ring the bell? *(Looking at each other.)* -" No, Sir." « That fire will be out." *(Mum.)* Off anew. "Dear! dear! the fire *is* out. " But O! that we could sketch him with his mild countenance, his elegant features, and his sweet smile, sitting with one leg twisted round the dounding to national honour. The chivalrous courtesy of Edward the Black Prince, is recorded as a great instance of moderation; and making allowance for the time at which he lived, it might be thought extraordinary, did we not recollect that the spirit of that period was chivalrous. Instances of condescension in the great, are collected with avidity, and extolled as above humanity. Yet what do we daily see? what is there that the members of the Royal Family do not do, when they can be serviceable, or even obliging? Does it not seem their wish to lay aside every impediment to their being useful? Is there an hospital for disease, is there a charitable institution which may not hope for royal patronage and presence? And what would have been said years ago, to what I myself saw, and which nobody seemed to care about? The Duke of Clarence walking through the thickest mud of the street of Richmond, attending on the military funeral of a member of a provincial corps! other, as if fearing to occupy more space than was equitable; his person in-

clining forward, as if wanting strength to support his height, and his arms crossed over his bosom, or his hands locked together on his knee; his oblong gold-mounted snuffbox, taken from the waistcoat-pocket opposite his hand, and either remaining between his fingers or set by him on the table, but which was never used but when his mind was occupied on conversation; so soon as conversation began, the box was produced.

His manner of exciting mirth was the most gentlemanly, every line of his face smiled, but he was never tickled by his own excitation. All he said was too well digested to take him by surprise; his was heartfelt mirth, and it was *through* his countenance that it was visible.

I know no attraction so great as that of such a house as Mr. Langton's, where, in an evening, without crowd or ostentation, there was always the chance of falling in with persons whose reception there, was a certificate in their favour. Compared with it, how *sensibly dull,* if I may use the expression, are those gregarious meetings where to stare, or make stare, is the highest aim. o

In some points, I wish Lady Rothes were imitated: it was her care to put every body at ease; it was her delight to break the barrier of strangership; and it was her habit to bring forward any one whom there was the least chance of overlooking. She made one person an attraction to another, and she sate amongst her friends as the superintendant of their comfort.

But I must not forget that my readers have not as lively a pleasure as I may have in recollecting these scenes which passed in the best years of impression. It is distinction to *me,* but of little avail to them, that under afflictions, or under the pressure of cares, I had the confidence of Mr. Langton and Lady Rothes. It is sweet to remember that neither time nor distance chilled or alienated them: *they* had no ill temper to be awakened, no pride to be galled, no caprice to need management, no selfishness to blind them; but they are gone, and in recollecting such friends, it is soothing to call to mind the promise we have that we shall not be detained for ever from them.

I am not so rich in my store of anecdotes, the contribution of Mr. Langton himself, as I might be; and of those which I owe to the survivors of the family, I dare not avail myself. It was the conversation of Mr. Langton indeed, that made me industrious in collecting, as it gave me a basis;' but he was no professed story-teller. "What he said flowed so naturally, and was so embedded in that which introduced it to his recollection, that to do justice to it, it would have required the preparations and resolutions of the chords in music.

The first thing I believe that I could *catc/i,* was the fact that Augustus King of Poland, father of Count Saxe , could tear two packs of cards. — This hero lives no longer in oral traditions j but he has taken his place in history. I suppose he "has had his day" in the decoration of sign-posts; but we English were not likely to exalt him in this way. We however honoured him by learning to dance the minuet, long after he was at rest in his grave, to a tune known by his name, and which was occasionally vulgarised by persons who tried to bring things down to their own comprehension, into "Marshal Saxby's, minuet."

In that very amusing work of M. Senac de Meilhan, the "Portraits and Characters of distinguished Persons of the latter part of the 18th Century," there is a curious trait of the r

And what of that? many will say. It sounds small indeed; but the small *purchase,* as it is termed, which such a body affords to the hand, renders it wonderful.

To the lovers of wonders, the ocular proof of such superiority of power affords a great treat; in the minds of many, it excites painful sensations, arising perhaps in the want of confidence of success without suffering. The man who lifted many hogsheads of water *in honour of Admiral Vernon,* was quoted to us when children, not for his prowess, but for the perfect want of connection between his exertion and the honour of the British admiral. I have heard my mother say that she saw an Irish gentleman

take up a small mahogany table of some solidity in his teeth. And to my horror I once beheld a young girl of no athletic frame lift by the ends of her long hair a very heavy leaden weight. I was in a situation where I could scarcely avoid seeing it, but I felt a wish that the girl would *jilt* the beholders.

soldierlike *nonchalance* of Marshal Saxe. — He kept his physician, M. Senac's father, always near his person, and took him in his carriage on his military services. At the siege of Tournay, he drove up close to the trenches, and, as if he had been going to make a call on a friend, said, on quitting the carriage, " I sha'n't be gone many minutes." M. Senac, who was very long-sighted, was convinced that he should remain within reach of a battery, on which he saw preparations making to fire. As the Marshal was alighting, he named to him the danger in which he would be left, TM Well," said he, "then pull up the glasses. "

How far we are to admire that *sang froid* which includes the concerns of our friends, is not quite a settled point. That which results not from stupidity or indifference, but from settled firm principles, cannot be too much admired.

When the fashion of embellishing history and inventing maniacs subsides, when adulterous sentiment and blasphemous poetry lose their charm, it might make a pretty variety to learn something of the world as it really is, from that sort of literature which interposes between biography and history.

The following I owe to Mr.Langton. When the Irish King at Arms waited on the then Bishop of Killaloe to summon him to parliament, which was a ceremony requiring the formality of the heraldic attire, the bishop's servant, not knowing what to make of his appearance, and not clearly comprehending the title with which his memory was charged, introduced him, saying, " My Lord, here is the King of Trumps."

When Goldsmith expressed an inclination to visit Aleppo, for the purpose of importing some of the mechanical inventions in use there, Dr. Johnson said, "Goldsmith will go, and he will bring

back a frame for grinding knives, which he will think a convenience peculiar to Aleppo." After he had published his "Animated Nature," Johnson said, "You are not to infer from this compilation, Goldsmith's knowledge on the subject; if he knows that a cow has horns, it is as much as he does know."

On this it is apposite to remark the exalted idea which we entertain in early life, of the intellectual acquisitions of writers. We fancy that what they tell must be written from the dictation of their own memory. When we have more experience, we find that there is often as much work for the *feet* as for the *fingers,* in the committing a few pages to paper, and that the claim to admiration is founded rather in knowing where to seek what we want than in possessing it. Enviable indeed are the few who carry their libraries in their heads.

Of the two following, I had the former from

Mr. Langton, and the latter my father had from

Mr. Cadell.

Goldsmith happened once to stop at an inn on the road, in a parlour of which was a very good portrait, which he coveted, believing it a Vandyke; he therefore called in the mistress of the house, asked her if she set any value on that old-fashioned picture, and finding that she was wholly a stranger to its worth, he told her it bore a very great resemblance to *his aunt* Salisbury, and that if she would sell it cheap, he Would buy it. A bargain was struck, a price infinitely below the value was paid. Goldsmith took the picture away with him, and had the satisfaction to find, that by this scandalous trick he had indeed procured a genuine and very saleable painting of Vandyke's.

Soon after Goldsmith had contracted with the booksellers for his History of England, for which he was to be paid five hundred guineas, he went to Cadell, and told him he was in the utmost distress for money, and in imminent danger of being arrested by his butcher or baker. Cadell *r* immediately called a meeting of the proprietors, and prevailed on them to advance him the whole, or a considerable part of the sum which by the original agreement he was not entitled to till a twelvemonth after the publication of his work. On a day which Mr. Cadell had named for giving this needy author an answer, Goldsmith came, and received the money, under pretence of instantly satisfying his creditors. Cadell, to discover the truth of his pretext, watched whither he went, and after following him to Hyde-Park Corner, saw him get into a post-chaise, in which a woman of the town was waiting for him, and with whom, it afterwards appeared, he went to Bath to dissipate what he had thus fraudulently obtained.

Have I told of my father's being invited by Goldsmith to look at a book, in which was some information that might be useful to him, and instead of lending it to him, tearing out the leaves?

The late king himself told Mr. Langton this anecdote. — While North, afterwards Bishop of Winchester, was at Eton, he was one day caught in his room, making quince-marmalade, for which, as against all rule, the then master punished him, by obliging him to make Greek verses, including the recipe for the marmalade. "No bad thought," added his Majesty, "but I did not think had had so much humour; for you know he is a stupid fellow."

"Whether I owe the following to Mr. Langton himself, or received it through the medium of one of the family, I do not recollect, but it is Mr. Langton's story.—A man was observed every Saturday, duly, and nearly at the same hour, to pass along a street in London, carrying an old paper hat-box under his arm. An inhabitant of the street, determined to find out what the box contained, came upon him abruptly, and contrived to run against the box, so as to make it discover its contents. *Coals* dropt out, and he said to the carrier of them, "Heyday! do you fetch coals in a hat-box?" "Yes," said the man, " I like to have them fresh and fresh."

This I presume was not intended as wit or humour, it was the apology of genteel poverty: but it was impossible to deny the praise of humour to a reply

I heard given, a short time since, in a country-town, to a little pert girl, who for the sake of calling out the oddity of an eccentric man, took pains to make him hear her, while he was employed amongst bottles in a wine-vault. Her natural home was a baker's shop just by. The weather being very warm, she called out, " Isn't it very hot Mr. down there?" "Not half so hot as in your oven, Miss Roll-y Poll-y," he replied.

Specimens of local wit or peculiarity I must postpone.

I confess myself indebted to one of the family for this admirable axiom of Mr. Langton's, which he impressed on the minds of his children, " The next best thing to knowing, is to be sensible that you do *not* know."

To Dr. Johnson himself I owe the following anecdotes respecting Mr. Langton's father, who, though I believe as little wanting in intellect as in morals, exhibited on some occasions curious instances of that inability to comprehend common things, which seems rare only because observation is not accurate. Of his goodness it is a proof, that he never left his chamber in a morning, without adding to his devotions the repetition of that excellent summary of the duties of a Christian, which is contained in our Church Catechism. Of the defect I allude to, these facts are proofs. He had bestowed considerable pains on enlarging a piece of water on his estate, and was showing to some friends what he had achieved, when it was remarked to him, that the bank which confined the water, was in one place so low as not to be a security against its overflowing. He admitted that *to the eye* it might appear dangerous: but he said he had provided against such an accident, by having had the ground in that spot dug deeper to allow for it.

The other anecdote respected a legacy of 1000/., equally divided between himself and a person to whom he was indebted 100/. He consented that this debt should be deducted from his moiety; but when the deduction was made, and he saw the person to whom he was indebted, with 200/. more than he had, he could not admit it just, that when

the other legatee was to have only 100/. from him, he should yet be 200/. the richer. And when an attempt was made to demonstrate it by figures, he could acquiesce no farther than to say it might be *true on paper,* but it could not be so in practice.

I find in a note-book, a better account of Mr. Langton's last days, than I can give from memory. I owe it to Dr. Mackie, whom, in 1812, I found at Southampton, where he was in the first estimation and practice as a physician, and certainly one of the most agreeable conversationists that his' luminous country sends amongst us. To Mr. Langton, he must have been invaluable, for he knew him, and appreciated him, and regretted that acquaintance began only when life was closing. Our friend, he said, had settled himself in one of two good houses, in a part of the town called Anspach Place, between the walls and the sea, and near the warm baths. His death he described, alas! as hardly in the course of nature, and this any one might have thought, who knew the longevity of his mother, his strong resemblance to her, and the general opinion that a figure so light of flesh bids fair to remain long in existence. But he had for some time complained of feeling himself weak, and what he descriptively called "overtopped," and wisely considered this as a warning of approaching dissolution. On my knowledge of him, I should very much doubt whether he took sufficient sustenance; I have said that the least call on his intellects would make him neglect his plate at dinner, and I should as soon have expected to see Milton's "sociable spirit" indulging hunger, as Mr. Langton. In short, though I should excite merriment were I to call him "an angel of a man," I am persuaded that all his inactivity, all the repugnance he showed to putting on the harness of this world's toil, arose from the spirituality of his frame of mind. And this I should still suppose, were it even to be proved (which I do not know that it can be,) that he ever gave way to anger. I believe his mind was in Heaven, wheresoever he corporeally existed.

In this state of declining strength he caught a catarrhal cold, so slight, that though Dr. Mackie was attending him, he did not mention it. A cough followed, which he soothed with Paregoric Elixir.

I should be cautious in naming the specific medicine, lest I might deter others from having recourse to it, but when I add from Dr. Mackie's report, that in the course of one night's disturbed rest, he took in small portions to the amount of two ounces, I need not fear depriving the world of invalids of a very useful medicine.

I was called out of my bed one morning at three o'clock, to attend to my mother who was taken very ill. Standing by her, while learning from her that she had taken some rhubarb and magnesia at going to bed, I accidentally cast my eye on the phial. What was my consternation, to perceive on the label, "Paregoric Elixir!" I however avoided alarming her, but sent to the apothecary, and in the meantime endeavoured to make light of the mistake. She had taken two ounces at a draught!—But as no time was lost in ascertaining the fact, the danger was soon removed. She, however, was for four months as weak as if she had had a very severe illness.

A worse mistake was that of a lady, who took hartshorn in the same quantity. It is of no use to repeat cautions or to inspire terror; but the blunders of servants and the heedlessness of professional persons ought never to be palliated. A ludicrous mistake occurred once to an *amateur* violin-player, who got hold on a piece of diachylon instead of resin. And a very harmless precipitancy of this kind is told me by a friend. A humane neighbour interested for a poor man, then very ill, ordered his man to send him a family bottle of castor oil. By mistake, a bottle of ketchup was sent, but the patient recovered. I have heard of one of those provincial practitioners, who arc

This excess so inflamed and obstructed the organs of respiration, that unable as he was to bear reducing, he expired in a few days.

It is well known that he was interred in the venerable church of St. Michael, in Southampton, with Johnson's celebrated wish, "Sit anima mea cum Langtono," on a marble tablet near the spot.

A cast taken after his death exists, in the possession of a clergyman, at Southampton, but such reminiscences are not of a nature to give pleasure, eventof the melancholy species.

I wish I could recover without more expense of time than I can afford, a mOst curious statement, which I believe appeared in the Gentleman's Magazine, of the ceconomy of an uncle of Mr. Langton's, whose income, if I am not mistaken, did not consulted far and near in great cases, and whose wife conversing with a lady on the medicines ranged in sight, said, "We mind none but the Baccadore medicines; it is to them we trust." What were Baccadore medicines? Those which stood on a shelf at the *back of the door* of this dispensary. exceed 200/. per annum, but to whom I have heard him say, his family were obliged for bequests. It might have served for imitation, or at least to show what *may* be done by good husbandry. The boasted man of Ross was of princely affluence and relaxed habits, compared with this younger son of a family, who, though possessing a considerable landed property, had, as is generally to be observed, demands on it in proportion to its power of satisfying them. The Man of Ross, with 500/. a year, did as much by his influence, as by his wealth; and though the axiom, *"Qui facit per alium, facit per se,"* holds good, there is some difference of computation required in directing the expenditure of another and contracting to the utmost our own.

I ought to have found a better place for an anecdote, which I had from the late Countess of Waldegrave. Mr. Langton told her, of Burke, that in conversation he uttered this sentiment, "How extraordinary it is, that /, and Lord Chatham, and Lord Holland, should each have a son so superior to ourselves!"

I should be ungrateful to one of those frequenters of our house, to whom I was most obliged, if I passed in silence the recollection of Mr. afterwards Dr. Henley, who on his compelled retreat from "William and Mary College in Virginia, where he had a professorship, brought a letter of introduction to Sir J. H. from a distant relation of our family, at that time engaged in the education of the then governor's sons, and by his office detained longer there.

Mr. Henley was received, as was due, with an invitation to dine; and the situation of American politics having deprived him of employment, he offered my father any assistance he could render to the work in which he found him engaged. I had no *jealousy* of this partnership, for my abilities at that time, alas! were far short of what Mr. Henley could do in translating, but my *pride* might have been wounded, had not his kind recognition of me, as employed on the same subject, made his superiority sit easily on my feelings.

He was, I believe, a native of Exeter, at least

Exeter seemed his home at the time, but his father, whom he mentioned as the captain of a trading vessel, was just then a prisoner, I think in France. He had been originally brought up a Presbyterian; and I have heard him speak of an awkwardness into which his want of familiarity with the service of the established church, betrayed him, on the first day of his preaching. It was at the Charterhouse Chapel, where he was encouraged to try his powers under the friendship of Dr. Nicholls, then the preacher there. Forgetting that part of the communion-service which intervenes between the morning-prayer and the sermon, he was quitting the pew while the *Jirst* psalm was singing; and before Dr. and Mrs. Nicholls were aware of it, had ascended a step or two to the pulpit. No sign from the Doctor was of use, to call to him was too indecorous; but the pew being near enough to reach him at one point, Mrs. Nicholls got hold on his gown. He, occupied with his situation, and conceiving that his gown had somewhere fastened itself, endeavoured to disengage it by pulling. Mrs. N. therefore was forced to increase her power of impeding; fortunately he looked round to see what so hindered him; and this terminated the distress of all parties.

He was a man of feelings much too warm; but this I should pass over, were it not to introduce with the mention of this inconvenience, the contrasting suavity of his manners, and the ingratiating modulation of his voice. To his failing he was very sensible, and was then duly sensible of his obligation, when it was controlled by his friends. Of this he gave a proof once, in speaking of an occurrence on the preceding evening at Vauxhall Gardens. He had paid what was demanded for the refreshments his party had taken, when presently a shilling was returned to him as bad : I know not whether any aliments so plebeian as cold beef and ham, are served in Vauxhall Gardens now, when, as I am told, they rival any descriptions in the " Arabian Nights' Entertainments," but I remember Sir J. H. 's relishing highly the humour of a waiter who with a most significant look pointed out the very small quantity of these commodities allowed for money, by his caricatured anxiety to preserve a plate in his hand from the influence of a gentle evening breeze.

My father was fond of Vauxhall. The band was good, and he had at any time the command of the instrumental music. It was indeed worth something to *see* the kettle-drums beat by Nelson: when I saw Lord Sandwich in the same situation, the poverty of his Lordship's performance excited my conhe had seen the waiter change one of those which he had given him; and the indignation he felt was tempt; but I ought to have considered that Nelson's grand attitudes and unembarrassed flourishes would have very ill become thirst Lord of the Admiralty. But in no performance on these deep-toned satellites of music, have I ever seen or heard what Nelson exhibited or contributed.

If we enumerate contrasts and inconsistencies, very high in any graduated catalogue must stand those connected with the existence of Vauxhall, as a place of public amusement. There is no need to go back to the time when it was

Sir Samuel Morland's residence; "his son," as Mr. Evelyn relates, "built a large room in the garden, much admired, on which was a Punchinello holding a dial." This convenient accommodation for company, to say nothing of Punch, might make it attractive to Mr. Jonathan Tyers, who purchased it, and made it a place of morning resort, which it continued to be, till the government interposed a wholesome prohibition of this ruinous scheme for getting rid of the most useful hours of the day, of which I have heard my mother say that its fascination left it utterly impossible for those who yielded to it, to conclude the day with any thing less idle.

But what I would remark is the total exchange of principles, ideas, and property, which the founder of this place made in taking to it. He had laid out a vast deal of money on his place near Dorking, where he had made a garden of the most melancholy kind, fit scenery for nothing but Young's "Night Thoughts." I remember when I was a girl, seeing a manuscript account of it; it was to a young mind rendered appalling, by. the conversion of that which is proverbially charming, into something little differing from the awful repositories of the dead.
fair. "My coat was half off," said he, "to give the rascal a thrashing, and well it was for me, that one of my friends stopt me."

To make this exchange, and to indulge the public with that which must tend to obliterate every idea impressed by his original work, Mr. Tyers sold property the most valuable, part of it peculiarly so, being rents guaranteed by the Exchequer; his vegetable charnel-house went into other hands, and I cannot find that any of its furniture remained. On no principle can such a violent change be accounted for, but on that of the operation of extremes; for certainly if there is one mode of making money less desirable than any other, it would be the maintaining a place of public admission.

Yet even on this spot, was to be found a being whose steadiness of conduct was entitled to the highest praise. The

questions to be resolved in a place of such resort, when Vauxhall was in high vogue as an evening-entertainment, brought my father and mother into some familiarity with a person whom I may justly term the *lady* who presented herself every evening in what was called "the bar." She was of superb beauty and the highest manners, a pattern of decorous dress, of great natural good sense, and, as will generally be found in those situations, possessing a most extensive knowledge of the world and its characters. Her justice to her employers, her oeconomy and prudence, entitled her to the highest praise; and the security every one felt under her attention, attracted many persons of distinction, to whom a mixed crowd might not have been agreeable. I have seen various personages of the Royal Family in conversation with her, and there was no one who frequented the gardens, who did not pay her respect. The system of management in the house was admirable; and such was her estimation, that even when retired to the quiet

He had a taste and talent for elegant poetry, and it is to be hoped that some of the very pretty things which he wrote have been preserved. I owed to him my acquaintance with the poetry of Dr. Beattie, and, perhaps, more on other subjects of literature than I can recollect; for his visits were frequent, his acquirements were considerable, and he very freely communicated what he had acquired. I remember it being jocularly said of him, that his "geese were all swans;" but in our judgments at that time this was no fault, at least it was a fault on the side most agreeable, and far better at all times than that calculating depreciation that makes geese of swans.

We lost much of his society by his going to reside at Cambridge, but my mother's hospitable disposition made our house his place of refresh enjoyment of her well earned ease and independence, she was not given up by her friends. She lived to a good old age, the pride of an affectionate family, and died with the comfortable consciousness of having borne with fortitude the evils of life, and of having done her duty in the station which vicissitudes had allotted her. One of the many proofs that it is to be imputed to ourselves alone, if in any state of life we are not respectable.

ment whenever he could reach us. New views opened on him. A young lady to whom he had been very seriously attached in Virginia, arrived in England at a time when he had the offer of the situation of tutor to two young gentlemen of one of the first families of these kingdoms. They were to be educated at Harrow, and there he took a house. He married and settled there, with every certainty that this mutable world can give, of permanent happiness and increasing advantages f; A ludicrous, but vexatious accident occurred to him in one of his visits to London. It was at a time when the lightness of the gold coinage required attention, and guineas short of weight were called in. To accommodate the shopkeepers of Cambridge, he offered to convey their light gold, and his good-nature brought him many applications. He was charged with a great quantity of coin, but by bad management it had come into contact with his linen, and he had none that was not cut by it. t I have often admired the wise check to precipitate resolutions which is contained in the saying, "Let no man say I will never drink of this water." And even what are called the chances of this, prove how imprudent it is to trust that such or such things cannot happen. As much rashness is there in despondency, as to those things which we may wish, but cannot expect will happen. Mrs. Henley came from a distant quarter of the globe, perfectly a stranger.

My mother had had in her childhood a playfellow, the but "Hope told a flattering tale." In the course of a year he was indeed a father, but it was only to know the sorrow of losing both wife and child.

He married again, and then settled in Suffolk, where his patron, the father of his pupils, had given him a living; but his situation there grew uncomfortable, and he made himself rather conspicuous by singularities of proceeding in circumstances of provincial litigation, under which it probably was difficult to

know what was the best course, and the event of which might, perhaps, be the rule on which the judgment of his conduct might be framed. I own I was extremely surprised to find him afterwards at the head of an institution requiring, I should have thought, qualities of temper, and a character of mind, diametrically opposite to his, but those must have known best who appointed him. grand-daughter of Sir Josiah Child, who built Wanstead House. Of this young lady, she, in early youth, lost sight, knowing only that she had married a gentleman in the army. In our first visit to Mr. Henley on his marriage, accident discovered to Lady H., that his newly married wife was the daughter of her former playfellow.

My brother Henry, who could best appreciate him as a scholar, says, that he was a good classic, and that he had in his last situation made progress in a work, by which he designed to settle ancient chronology with improved certainty.

On one occasion Mr. Henley was an instance of what I have said of the father of Mr. Langton. He had remained ignorant of that which is a matter of almost general knowledge, and this raised a good-humoured laugh when, as one of the contributing annotators on Shakspeare, he furnished a conjecture, that in the passage, "Where the rabbit is kindled, there she dwells," we ought to read " kind led," that is to say, led by her kind, or in other words, I suppose, induced by others of her species.

But Henley, when he was a visitor at my father's, was, with all his peculiarities, so agreeable, that I can even now picture to myself, as a day of perfect conversational enjoyment, one in which Steevens should have been at the breakfasttable, Henley at dinner, and at the tea-table BENNET LANGTON.

314 ADDENDA.
I have said in this volume, that I considered the style of Sir J. H.'s Life of Johnson as not his own original style: it may be inferred from this that I cannot praise it. That it is far better than his daughter's, I willingly admit, and could, alas! bring many to testify; but I care for no

depreciation of myself, if I can but preserve from oblivion, two short tracts of his, which I have hinted my intention of bringing forward. The one, written on the apprehended dissolution of the Academy of Ancient Music, may now be read with revived interest, when that is doing which he would have rejoiced to see attempted; the other may, on any occurrence of a similar kind, bring forward useful facts, and at *every* time I think it will appear a masterly specimen of fair argument: placed here, they leave to all readers the option of perusing or disregarding them.

I wish I possessed some other of his argumentative compositions, particularly those which were called for by an attempt to remove the Fleet-Prison to the site of the venerable palace of the Bishops of Ely, recorded by Shakspeare (who that passes by Ely Place would now believe it?) for the strawberries produced in its gardens. The obnoxious removal would have placed all the Hatton estate within the rules of the prison; the interests of Lord Winchelsea, as well as of the parish, were involved, and they both testified their gratitude for their rescue.

Hatton Garden was then an esteemed situation for the gentry; no shops were permitted but at the lower end, and few parts of the town could vie with it. We lived in a part of it which afforded us, beside a wide street in front, and a sharp descent within a few yards, an opening behind overlooking a good garden, and, without the intervention even of a chimney, a view of the fields, where Pentonville was afterwards built: but this situation, like all others in succession, is ruined by trades and low associations. The progress of Fashion, as she shifts her town-residence, is worthy of observation, and would claim that only, were it not for the evils that accompany her march; but unfortunately, she looks with contempt on every thing she leaves behind her, and one glance of this description blasts the value of pro

Mr. Evelyn, in his Diary, records his going to London, June 7th, 1659, to see the foundations then laying, for a long street and buildings in Hatton Garden, designed for a little town, lately an ample garden.

Pennant mentions Hatton house and garden as having occupied the site of the orchard belonging to the palace of the Bishop of Ely. Sir Christopher Hatton, by his interest with Queen Elizabeth, it is well known to her shame, extorted this piece of ground from Cox then bishop.

perty. Next above Hatton Garden ranked Bedford Row, then arose Bedford Square, and then Russell Square, to the ruin of the excellent houses in Great Russell Street, Bloomsbury. The houses in Newman Street have been rendered a drug, and Berners Street is fast yielding up its dignity. But these are modern streets, and must take their chance. Squares, composed of fine family-mansions, and erections on the property of our first nobility, would, it may be supposed, keep up their aristocratic character; but it is not so. Milliners and other trades creep into the houses of those whose custom has furnished the requisite funds, and persons of fashion and figure, instead of standing their ground, yield and edge off to the north-west: built out there, they retire and retire, till their town houses are country villas. This is not in the spirit of that solid liberty of which our nation so boasts. It certainly does not savour of the opinion of Martial, in the spirited epigram which Cowley has, with equal spirit, translated in his "Would you be free?" But alas! the vice of this country, and of many others, is that spirit of discontent which makes us all covet that which we have not: possessed, the fancied good again takes the place of the fancied ill; and to all this there is no end, but in the usual punishment of such covetousness, the destruction of the thing coveted, and of those who covet it.

I regret, also, that I have not Sir J. H. 's charge to the grand jury of Middlesex, after the dreadful riots of 1780, a period of which I have yet to speak. But regret is vain; I must rest content with what I have.

Priority of date demands precedence for "the Case of the County of Middlesex, with respect to the Gaol of Newgate."

Though I cannot give the precise date of this paper, its purpose will, in some measure, ascertain it, as it was written in defence of the county, against the demands of the city, when it was first in agitation to take down the old prison of Newgate, which was done in 1776, and rebuild it in a more eligible place. To such a proceeding no one could reasonably object, but with that part of the argument my father had no concern; he was intrusted with the defence of his county against a demand, the justice of which was to be decided; he stated the case, and it had its proper effect.

"The gaol of Newgate is, and for upwards of 600 years hath been, a common prison and place of security for felons and other offenders; and, so far as it tends to secure and bring to punishment those who, by acts of rapine and violence, endanger the persons and properties of mankind, it seems to be of public use and benefit; notwithstanding which, the citizens of London, and several tradesmen inhabiting near the said gaol, have of late laboured to represent it as a most dangerous nuisance.

"To induce a general acquiescence in this opinion, they suggest that the said gaol is ill constructed, close and incommodious, and unfit for the reception of prisoners. That a great number of prisoners have been usually crowded into the said gaol at the opening of every sessions. That the prisoners have frequently been visited with a malignant disease, call the gaol-distemper, whereby the health of all persons resorting to the sessionshouse must be endangered. That the said gaol cannot be rendered healthy and commodious, without being taken down and rebuilt on a more extended plan. They suggest further, that of the number of 1000 prisoners yearly committed to Newgate, two-thirds are the prisoners of the county; and from thence would seem to insinuate, that the expense of rebuilding the said gaol (which, according to their own estimates, will amount to 40,000/.) should be borne by the county and city in the proportion of two to one.

"In order to avoid so heavy a charge,

and to prevent the entailing on themselves and posterity, the burthen now attempted to be laid on them, the inhabitants of the county of Middlesex think it incumbent on them to state the following facts, submitting the arguments deduced therefrom, to the judgment of candid and impartial men.

"They say, that the gaol of Newgate is supposed to have been originally built in the reign of King Henry I., or of King Stephen, that is to say, between the years 1100 and 1154, and that the same hath been under the sole government of, and hath from time to time, sometimes by express mandate from the king, as in the 6th year *of* Edward II., been rebuilt, repaired, altered, and enlarged, by the citizens of London; the consequence whereof is, that they are bound perpetually to repair it, and would be punishable at law if they did not.

"They further say, that supposing the number of prisoners yearly committed to the said gaol, to be as great as is alleged, the number is not greater now than it hath been for a series *of* years past, during which, no application to charge the county with any expense attending Newgate hath ever been made. That county prisoners are secured in that prison is admitted; but that more than a few, compared with those who are confined in the prisons of the county, and tried at the Hicks's Hall sessions, are sent thither by the justices, is absolutely denied t and how fallacious that method of estimation must be, which represents the prisoners sent to Newgate by the county, as two to one of the London prisoners, will appear by the following state of facts. The county have several gaols, to which those charged with petty larcenies.

I and misdemeanors of all kinds are committed, as are also prisoners for felonies and other offences, properly triable at the Old Bailey. That this is the general practice is notorious, and if, perhaps, once in fifty times, the county magistrates find it necessary to deviate from it, by committing offenders of the latter class, originally and immediately to Newgate, rather than to the other gaols, the exceptions are hardly worth opposing to the general rule; thus far with respect to commitments. As to gaol deliveries, it is to be noted that the county holds sessions at Hicks's Hall, eight times in the year, at which sessions the prisoners of the first class are tried; and take any one session in the year, it seldom happens that the prisoners so tried, are not double the number of those tried the same session at the Old Bailey. As to these latter, it has been said, that they are at first committed to the county prisons; there they are maintained at the county expense, and would remain till the instant of their respective trials, but that in obedience to an order of the Old Bailey session, made in May 1726, doubtless for the ease of the court, they are removed to Newgate six days before every session, which, at the Old Bailey are also held eight times in the year; and, after trial, that gaol, agreeably to the words of the Old Bailey commission, is delivered of such prisoners. Hence it appears that the city have the custody of such only of the Middlesex prisoners as are triable at the Old Bailey, for six days before, and during every session, and these very seldom hold a week each. Suppose, then, we estimate their time of keeping such prisoners at a fortnight for each session, it will follow that four months in the year is the utmost time for which, with truth, the city may be said to have the custody of county prisoners, unless sometimes by accident, a few may wait for transportation. The allegation of a proportion of two to one against the city, would lead a stranger to the belief, that the county had no gaols of their own, and that, all the year through, and without any intermission, the justices were sending in prisoners to Newgate, in the proportion above mentioned, and that the city keep them as long as they do their own prisoners. The facts above stated are the truth of the case, and the fallacy of the charge is apparent.

"Here it may be observed, that that respectful obedience which the county have always paid to the order of the Old Bailey session, is what the citizens mean, when they complain that the county prisoners are crowded into their gaol.

"The county of Middlesex have two prisons, besides Tothill-Fields Bridewell, which they built, and do maintain; and in these, though, except about sessions time, they are generally full, no malignant disease hath ever yet appeared, and had the same care been taken to prevent the accumulation of filth in Newgate, as hath been exercised in the county prisons, that malignant disease, of which the citizens so loudly complain, had very likely never appeared among them,

"But that an insinuation so alarming, as that the health of all persons resorting to the sessions-house must be in danger, may not go unanswered, it is necessary to be more particular, and to revert to a fact that it is extremely fitting the public should be acquainted with. On the 27th of April 1750, a great number of persons, attending the Old Bailey session, in a crowded court, and uncommonly warm weather, were seized with a fever, communicated as is generally supposed, by the infection of the Newgate prisoners, of which disease to the number of about forty persons, among whom were two of the King's Judges and the Mayor of London, lost their lives.

"The late Sir Michael Foster, one of the Judges of the Court of King's Bench, has thought fit to perpetuate the memory of this disastrous event, in a volume of Reports, published by himself; and, enquiring into the causes of it, assigns for one the filthiness of the gaol, and the avenues *to* it. This misfortune did indeed awaken the attention of the city, and led the magistrates into a survey of the prison in which the seeds of this infection had long been treasured up. The consequence of this survey was a discovery of a vast quantity of filth, which had been many years accumulating in the several apartments of the prison, of such various kinds, as left very little room to doubt of the causes of that contagion, to which the above calamity was owing. Upon this the city set about a work, which it would have been happy if they had thought of sooner: viz. the cleansing the prison; the filth was collected together, and, for very obvious reasons, the night was chosen as the properest time for its removal to some distance from the town; and to one, or other of the adjacent fields, it was carried by cartloads, and buried, and, through the Providence of God, since that time, no such misfortune has happened. Thus, however plausibly the citizens may argue from the supposed danger of infection, from a distemper to which the gaol of Newgate is said to be subject, it seems that that danger may be averted by methods less expensive, than a total demolition of the fabric.

"The city affect to consider their connection with the county as a burthen on them: whether it is so, or not, let their own charters speak. By these it appears that they are possessed of many valuable privileges, in consequence of this connection: and it is a known maxim in law, *Qui sentit commodum, sentire debet onus.* In some of the most antient of their charters, the citizens are declared to hold the shrievalty of Middlesex together with that of London, in farm; and, to adopt the metaphor, a most profitable farm it has proved to them; for, to go no farther back than the year 672, it ap pears by accounts produced by themselves, that the sums received by the city, to excuse persons nominated by the Mayor, from serving the office of Sheriffs of London and Middlesex, amount to upwards of 148,750*l.* The connection between the office of sheriff and a place of security for the persons of those whose escape from justice he is at law answerable for, does very naturally point out a method of applying the sums above shown to have been raised, which had it been attended to, would have rendered the present attempt unnecessary. The citizens might have reasoned in this way: money has been raised by sheriffs' fines; the strength. of the prison is the sheriffs' security; let, therefore, the person who serves the office avail himself of the default of him who has declined it; and let the money so raised be a fund for the maintenance of that prison, without which no man could serve it at all. But whether the city ever reasoned thus or not, can only be guessed from the methods which of late years have been practised, as well in the raising, as the disposing of fines for that office. The inhabitants of the county do not think themselves concerned to enquire, whether or no the supreme magistrate of the city has a right to the nomination of this officer; a right, if it be one, that from the manner in which they had seen it exercised, seems to include in it a power little less than that of raising money on the subject, whenever, and to what amount he pleases. They cannot, however, omit to observe, that such a power as this, with all due deference be it spoken, the law has never intrusted to the kings of this realm: on the contrary, the best of them have ever disclaimed it; and they are inclined to think that nothing can sanctify such an extraordinary privilege, but the exertion of it for the general and not a partial good, and that too in a degree consistent with equity and moderation.

"But why, say the city, must we take upon ourselves the charge of any of the county prisons? The answer is, Because upon your own repeated solicitations, ye have obtained what no other city in the kingdom possesses, the power of nominating, not barely your own sheriffs, but a sheriff for your neighbours; and though this power is no injury to the county, it is evident that the burthen of which ye so much complain, is no other than the necessary consequence of your uniting those two distinct offices, and the several jurisdictions attendant thereon in the same persons: the prison for London is situate in, and is one of the gates *of* the city; the sessions of gaol delivery for Middlesex, are held in London for the convenience of the city; the Middlesex prisoners can therefore be tried no where but in London: the court sends for such of them as are triable at the Old Bailey (and they, as has been shown, are but a small proportion of the whole number of county prisoners), in order for trial, and the sheriff, for his own security, keeps them in Newgate, the city prison, as a place of the greatest strength and safety. Is not all this the act of the city? Are not the county in this respect absolutely pas-

sive? With what face of truth, then, is it ventilated abroad, that the county crowd their prisoners on the city? or can any rational conclusion be deduced from these premises to charge the county with the expenses attending the prison of Newgate in any proportion whatever?

"And it seems that, at some times, the citizens themselves entertain the same opinion of the matter, viz. that the county have nothing to do with Newgate; for they dispose of the places of the keeper and ordinary; and, in two instances, have they assumed the right of nominating a clerk of the arraigns, for the trial of the county prisoners; and not to mention that they have altered, enlarged and improved the gaol, till at last, as they themselves say, it is become a most dangerous nuisance, they never thought it at all necessary to advise with the county as to its construction; some few years ago they insured the prison from fire, in their own names, in the Hand in Hand Fire Office; soon after a fire happened therein; they applied to the office, received 500l., and laid it out as they thought fit.

"In all matters relating to the government or management of the prison, the citizens have constantly exercised their own judgment, without consulting the county; and whenever it has been necessary to apply to the great council of the nation, they have done it alone and without the intervention or concurrence of the county; and of this a very remarkable instance shall now be given.

"Immediately after the dreadful conflagration in 1666, in which the greater part of the city was consumed, the citizens thought it necessary to implore the aid of parliament, to enable them to rebuild their public edifices: at that time it was never pretended that the county were chargeable with any part of the expense of rebuilding Newgate; and the parliament were so little disposed to think so, that by an act of 19 Car. II. they granted the city a duty arising from coals brought into the port of London, which is expressly appropriated, among other things, to the rebuilding of gaols for felons. Enabled by this grant, which

by their own account, produced 736,804l., the citizens rebuilt, among other public edifices, the greater part of the now gaol of Newgate, and to intimate how little they thought the county had to do with it, they stamped it with the city arms, and by inscriptions on the east and west front of the gate, commemorated the aera of its re-edification, and the names of the magistrates under whose government it was begun and completed, in terms that import little less than a sole and exclusive property in it.

"Here it is proper to mention, that by a charter of 1 Henry IV., that king grants to the citizens of London, the keeping as well of the gates of Newgate and Ludgate, as of all other gates and posterns of the said city. When this grant has been urged as a proof that the gates, and Newgate in particular, belong to the city, the answer has been, that they claim nothing more under it, than the bare custody of the gates; and yet the city have taken upon them to pull down all the city gates, but this of Newgate; and, besides selling the materials, they have converted their respective scites into freehold estates, which they have let upon leases, reserving to the city large fines and ground rents; and, doubtless, they would have acted in the same manner by Newgate, if they had not had something farther in view.

"The unhappy situation of the county of Middlesex is such as almost to environ the city of London, and one of the consequences of this situation is, that the numerous poor, which from the most remote parts of the kingdom, are attracted to the metropolis, though the city have the benefit of their labour, as having their residence mostly in the circumjacent parishes, become legally settled in those parishes, and so commence a burthen on the county: hence the difference between the poor's rate in the city and suburb parishes; and, in all the improvements which of late years have been made of the city estates by building, the citizens have constantly had an eye to the accommodation of merchants and other principal traders, and seem to have forgot that, as well the poor as the rich, need houses to dwell in.

"Whatever colour maybe given to the complaints of the citizens, it is evident that the subject matter of those complaints is not a public concern, but simply a question between party and party, namely whether the city alone, or the city and county jointly, are to be at the expense of rebuilding Newgate. Upon what principle then would they have it determined? If upon legal ones, the county insist on a legal exemption from this burthen. If the equity of the case is to be the measure of justice, enough has been said to prove that the citizens have not performed that condition which alone could entitle them to the benefits of an equitable adjudication: In short, they have not done equity. But supposing they had, what is the equity they contend for? Why nothing more than that the city may retain the honours and advantages, and that the inhabitants of Middlesex may bear the burthen of the county magistracy; there will then be somewhat for each party.

"But the humanity of the public is appealed to; and if it were possible to find out any tribunal where mere humanity, unassisted by law or equity, can be supposed to preside, the county would willingly meet the citizens there, but they know of none such. That compassion is due to prisoners and captives, religion teaches, and the county admit; but that there is any precept which enjoins the exercise of this virtue in an equal degree by all to all, they deny. In the present case, let it be remembered that the city, and not the county, built the gaol of Newgate, and that the citizens are the sole owners of it; and that if the distress of the prisoners confined there, be owing to the badness of its construction, the inhumanity of suffering that distress to continue, while the citizens are engaged in a hopeless contest with the county, is chargeable on those only to whom the gaol belongs.

"Not to combat any longer with shadows, it is most evident that there is not the least pretence for imposing on the county, any part of the expense of rebuilding the gaol of Newgate; it remains now to show how little the city are entitled, in this respect, to the aid of the public.

"By the several sums above shown to have been received by the citizens, it appears that they have been possessed of at least two funds, amounting to near a million sterling, out of which, if they had thought fit, they might have rebuilt their goal long ago, without the aid of parliament, or any contribution of the county; and if they are not at present very well able to do it, it must be owing to some reasons which the public are strangers to, and which it is high time they were made acquainted with. In 1720, the offices sold by the city were estimated at 152,000Z. by one of their favourite historians: the revenues of the city are immense; and a very few years will put it in the actual possession and receipt of such an estate, as must yield an income much more than adequate to all the expenses of its government. As the sources of these revenues are, in general, royal grants, many of them under the express condition of well governing the city, they are enjoyed by the citizens, in their political and corporate capacity; the revenues arising from these grants, cannot be considered as matters of private emolument, or the right of individuals; in reason and justice, they are destined for public purposes, such as the erection and repair of gaols, bridges, and other public edifices; and, till these resources fail, which it is hardly possible they should ever do, it is humbly apprehended, that in respect of a prison so peculiarly their own, as this of Newgate has been shown to be, the citizens have not the least pretence of claim to the bounty of the public."

The little tract which follows, requires no introduction to render its history or its design intelligible. I have already done what is in my power to keep alive the memory of that parent society to which the most gratifying of all the concerts of the metropolis owes its existence. To prevent the dissolution of this primitive establishment, Sir J. H. printed and liberally distributed, what he entitled An Account of the Academy of Antient Music.

"The Academy of Antient Music, at the Crown and Anchor Tavern, in the Strand, was instituted about the year 1710, by a number of gentlemen, performers on different instruments, in conjunction with some of the most eminent masters of the time. The design of this establishment was to promote the study and practice of vocal and instrumental Most justly did a lady say of two of our friends, whose taste led them to these feasts of the ear, " They were not in *this* world when such music was performing." harmony; in order to which, the foundation of a library was laid, consisting of the most celebrated compositions, as well in manuscript as in print, that could be procured, either at home or abroad.

"Under the direction of the late Dr. John Christopher Pepusch, whose memory will be ever revered by all lovers of music, and with the assistance of Mr. Galliard, Dr. Maurice Greene, Mr. Bernard Gates, and the gentlemen and boys of St. Paul's Cathedral, and the Chapel Royal, the academy continued in a very flourishing state, till about the year 1728, when Dr. Greene thought proper to leave it, and set up an academy at the Devil Tavern, Temple Bar, which subsisted but a few years.

"The secession of Dr. Greene and his dependants, was not such an injury to the academy, as it was feared it would prove: they left it, it is true, but they left it in peace; and the members of which it was composed, in consequence of the loss they had sustained, became emulous to excel each other in their endeavours to promote its interests, and to disseminate the love of harmony throughout the kingdom.

2

"With these assistances, and that which the academy derived from the performance of the amiable Henry Needier, Esq., who for many years led the orchestra, the late Earl of Abercorn, Mr. Mulso, Mr. Millan, Mr. Dobson, and many other gentlemen, who were excellent performers, it continued to nourish until the year 1734, when Mr. Gates retired, and drew off with him the children of the Chapel Royal.

"In the interval between the secession of Dr. Greene, and Mr. Gates, viz. in the month *of* February 1731-2, the academy had given a signal proof of the advantages arising from its institution. The oratorio of Esther, originally composed for the Duke of Chandos, was performed in character by the members of the academy, and the children of the Chapel Royal; and the applause with which it was received, suggested to Mr. Handel, the thought of exhibiting that species of composition at Covent Garden theatre; and to this event it may be said to be owing, that the public have not only been delighted with the hearing, but are now in possession of some of the most valuable works of that great master.

-"The loss which the academy sustained by the secession of some members, the death of others, and above all, by the want of boys, laid them under great difficulties, and drove them to the necessity of trying what could be done without the assistance of treble voices; but the experience of one season drove them to the alternative of an increased expence, or annihilation. In this predicament, they resolved upon an expedient that should not only make good the loss they had sustained, but convey a benefit to posterity. In short, they determined upon such an establishment, and such a subscription, as would render the academy at once a society for the entertainment of its members, and a seminary for the instruction of youth in the principles of music, and the laws of harmony. Invitations to parents, and offers of such an education for their children, as would fit them as well for trades and businesses, as the profession of music, were given by advertisements in the public papers: these brought in a great number of children, and such of them as were likely to be made capable of performing the soprano parts in vocal compositions, were retained. Dr. Pepusch generously undertook the care of their instruction for a stipend, the largest the academy could afford, though greatly disproportionate to his merit, and succeeded so well in his endeavours to improve them, that some of the most eminent profes-

sors of the science owe their skill and reputation to his masterly method of tuition.

"A subscription of two guineas, and a resolution to admit auditors as members, enabled the managers to carry this their benevolent design into execution j they enriched their collection with such a variety of compositions, as rendered it, even then, perhaps, the most valuable repository of musical treasure in Europe. Abbate Steffani transmitted to them from Hanover, the most valuable of his works from time to time, as they were composed. Mr. Handel and Signor Geminiani lent the academy their countenance, the latter frequently honouring it with his own exquisite performance and it continued to flourish till the year 1752, when it sustained a loss which will long be deplored, in the death of Dr. Pepusch, and which was far from being repaired by his generous benefaction to it, of the most valuable part of his library.

"Soon after this melancholy event, some of the members of the academy, reflecting, on the great encouragement given to concerts, thought it might tend to the interests of the society, to give it a new form, and by engaging some of the most excellent performers on particular instruments, derive assistance to it as a concert, from persons who might be apt to disregard it as an academy. But here they were involved in a new difficulty: the great increase of late years in the number of places of public diversion, and the consequent increase in the demands of eminent performers, made it impossible, even with a subscription of two guineas and a half, to continue a competition against greater resources than private contribution, and they now find, that these latter are not adequate to the expence of the plan which they last adopted.

"The members of the academy therefore find themselves reduced to the necessity of recurring to the principles of its first institution; and they desire, if possible, to perpetuate the existence of a society, calculated for the improvement of one of the noblest of the sciences, and the communication of rational and so-

cial delight; to which end they wish for the assistance of those, who profess to love and admire music, such as are susceptible of its powers, such in short as are capable of distinguishing between the feeble efforts of simple melody, and the irresistible charms of elegant modulation and well-studied harmony.

"The friends of this institution are sensible of the prejudices which its very name, The Academy of Antient Music,' may excite; and that those persons, who think no music can be good which is not new, will hardly be induced to join in the support of an establishment, professedly intended for the study and practice of that which is old.

"To obviate prejudices of this kind, little more is necessary than barely to state them: those now under consideration are reducible to the following two positions: —

"Nothing in music is estimable, that is not new. No music tolerable which has been heard before.

"In answer to which, it may be said, that this kind of reasoning is never applied to other intellectual gratifications; for no man was ever yet so weak as to object to the works of Virgil or Raffaelle, that the one wrote seventeen hundred, or that the other painted two hundred and fifty years ago.

"But, perhaps, nothing more is meant by the objection, than that the efficacy of music is abated by repetition.

"Not to enquire what kind of music that must be, the merit whereof evaporates in the performance, let it be asked, does any man forbear the perusal of an Epic Poem, merely because he has read it before? or does any admirer of painting or sculpture, withdraw his eye from a fine picture or statue, because it has once surveyed them? Nay, rather, does he not employ all his attention to explore their several beauties, and, in the exercise of a learned curiosity, find continual delight?

"Again, let it be asked, are these objections to the best music of the best times, founded in truth and experience? or are they the result of a vicious taste, and a depraved judgment? Much of the music now in the possession of the academy, is as new to us as it was to our fathers; and will any one in his sober senses assert, that they had not ears and rational souls as well as ourselves? or that those sweet interchanges of melody, those artful combinations of concordant sounds, which inspired such men as Shakspeare and Milton with the praises of this divine science, can at any time be heard with indifference by a nice and unprejudiced ear? If this be the. case, music, the principles whereof seem interwoven in the very constitution of the universe, is mere delusion, and the pleasure arising from it, resolvable into caprice, fashion, into any thing but reason and philosophy.

"Farther, let it be enquired, how far the love of novelty has contributed to the variety of music, and it will be found to have excluded some of the most valuable kinds of composition, and" thereby produced uniformity instead of variety.

"Every judge of music is aware of the effects of compositions in the minor third of the several keys, and that by the hearing of such, the sweetest sensations are excited; and the artful contexture of fugue and canon are the admiration of all who are skilled in the science: these two kinds of music are in danger of being lost; for the compositions of this day are almost solely in the major third, and their structure little better than divided counterpoint, and what is still worse, on a monotonic bass; nor are the compositions, which some affect to admire, less liable to the objection of uniformity in respect to their several divisions or Strains. For reasons, which no one is willing to avow, *adagio* music is exploded, and we are content to forego the majesty and dignity of the *largo* and *andante* movements, with all the variety arising from the interchange of different airs and measures, for the noise and rattle of an unisonous *allegro,* to which no name can be given, or the intoxicating softness of that too-often iterated air, the minuet.

"He that reflects on such instances of modern levity as these, and that the effect of new productions is such, as that no one pretends, or even wishes, to remember the music that pleased him

a month ago, may very reasonably demand who are the competitors with the composers of the last century, and the former half of the present; or of which of them can it be said, that his crudities are less evanescent than the form of a cloud, or that his most laboured studies have survived the fate of an almanac.

"But lest it should be imagined, than an unwarrantable fondness for antiquity is the.motive with the academy for the cultivation of antient music, they desire it may be understood, that they apply the epithet *antient* to the compositions of the sixteenth century, and that they carry their

" In order to understand the reason of this restriction, it is necessary to advert to the history of music, *which,* so far as is material to the present purpose, is this. About the year 1500, Gafurius, or as he is otherwise called, Franchinus, a native of Lodi in Italy, having with great pains and expence procured copies and translations of Aristides Quintilianus, Bacchius Senioris, Manuel Bryennius, Ptolemy, and others of the Greek musicians, and having thoroughly studied Boetius and Guido Aretinus, read lectures on music in the public schools of Mantua, Verona, Milan, and other provinces and cities in Italy. The Provencal *violars* and *musars* were almost the only composers and musicians of the preceding ages; but the knowledge of the science which Gafurius diffused throughout Italy, gave rise to a new species of composition, of which, under the patronage of the Roman pontiffs, Palestrina is supposed to have been the improver, if not the inventor, the nature whereof is best to be judged of by his motet, *'Exaltabo te Domine,'* and his no less excellent madrigal, *'Veramente in amore.'* He was organist and chapel-master of St. Peter's at Rome, and flourished about the year researches no farther back than the time when Palestrina and his contemporaries, those glorious luminaries of the musical world, attracted the admiration of the ablest judges, and that they have ever paid a sedulous attention to such productions as their intrinsic merit has, at any period, rendered wor-

thy of regard.

"After so much care and pains taken to enrich it, it will hardly be objected to the academy's collection of music, that it is deficient in variety; and when it is known that the countries of Italy, Germany, France, Spain, the Netherlands, and England, have severally contributed, and that very largely, to the forming it, very little dread will remain of that satiety or indifference which attends the hearing of music calculated for the present hour, and not intended for posterity. For, not to mention the great number of compositions which the academy are possessed of, even so great as that the youngest 1580. The improvements in music since his time, consist in the associating instruments with voices, and the invention of new combinations, which, without transgressing the laws of harmony, are supposed to be capable of an almost infinite variety." person now living might hope in vain to hear them all, nor that variety of style observable in them, which is the characteristic of different masters, every species of vocal and instrumental music is in its turn exhibited by the academy for the entertainment of its members: the general arrangement of these is into compositions for the church, the theatre, and the chamber; the first head includes masses, motets, anthems, hymns, and psalms; the second, oratorios, masques, serenatas, overtures, and concertos; and the third, madrigals, trios, duettos, and cantatas; to the true and just performance whereof, the academy have hitherto been, and with the assistance which they now solicit, trust they shall yet be, equal.

"The hopes of success in these their endeavours, arise from that propensity which they observe in people of this country, to the cultivation of the politer arts, and the general encouragement it affords to laudable pursuits. They behold, with pleasure, persons of the first rank in this kingdom associated for the improvement of a particular species of vocal harmony, and with exemplary munificence, dispensing rewards proportioned to the merits of such as are emulous to excel in it. Farther, they repose great confidence in the good sense of this nation, of which they have a convincing proof, in the respect which, for a succession of ages, has been paid to the works of our great dramatic poet of Elizabeth's days, whose best compositions, by the way, are as liable to reproach on the score of their antiquity, as any of those which the academy have long laboured to recommend. In short, they flatter themselves, that the studies of such men as Palestrina, Tallis, Bird, Carissimi, Colonna, Stradella, Purcell, Bassani, Gasparini, Latti, Steffani, Marcello, Buononcini, Pergolesi, Handel, Perez, and many others, abounding in evidences of the deepest skill and finest invention, when duly attended to, will be thought worthy the admiration of every musical ear, and afford a manly and rational delight to all the votaries of this noble science.

"A society founded on principles like these, can hardly fail of proving an inexhaustible fund of benefit and entertainment. Here the student in the musical faculty will find the means of forming his style after the most perfect models. Here the timid and modest performer may acquire that degree of firmness and confidence which is necessary for displaying his excellencies in public. Here the ingenuous youth, who prefers the innocent pleasures of music, to riot and intemperance, may taste of that mirth which draws no repentance after it; and hither may those repair, to whom the studies or labours of a day, must necessarily endear the elegant delights of a musical evening.

"Padre Paolo Sarpi resigned his breath with a prayer for the republic of Venice, which, it is to be hoped, every friend of the muses, applying it to the academy of antient music, will adopt; and in the words of that excellent man, cry out ESTO PERPETUA!" vW *amicissimum E. S. in novos labores incumbentem.*

Tu colas Phœbum, tibi quam benignum!
Victima et ccelos petat usque summos!
Duplici famam solidas opesque
Munere donat.

Te jubet celsum penetrare templum

Ter sacer Praeses Medicine, et almas
Grata vult Musas tibi serta nectant
Cuncta scientes.

Ipse Musarum pater atque rector.
Te decet verum colere et fovere,
Lumen, et multum populo petenti
Tendere, certi.

Nee lepos deerit tibi vindicanti
Crucis aut sanctum decus aut honores,
Illius leto gravia expiantis
Crimina mundi.

Annuant votis superi — salutem
Haud neget, Justus modo sit magister,
Sint boni, si fas, calami — papyrus
Integra, clara.

Amicum suum Aug. W; inter primes ob peritiam et fidelitatem in rebus forensibus agendis coUocandum ita ob leporem benigne missum H. H. salutat.

En tibi, juris veteris novique,
Per graves litis strepitus, perito,
Semper et fido timidis patrono
Dura querenteis.

Musa, nee stulte videatur audax,
Debitas solvit verecunda grates,
(Dum timet longo tua jam morari
Tempora versu,)

Nuper ob missum leporem nee alter,
Pulcrior mensae decus esse posset,
Sive furtivo feriatur ictu
Sive Dianas.

Praetor et sumat seniorve pellem,
Duplicet vestem pluviis Novembris
Quis velit sumat, bene — nos edamus
Sit modo carnem.

Apollo as the god of physic.

ATRAMENTO DEFICIENTI, *Latitiam Matildam Hawkins sic supplex aUoquitur*
H. *Hawkins.*

Praeses o nigri, mihi supplicanti
Grata sis sicco calamo, nee uti
Coge me plumbo, male quam ferenti
Temporis ictus!

Quanta sint nigri bona tu memento,
Dantis aeternas operi poetae
Splendido laudes, pereunte plumbo
Mox perituro.

Ne neges; primum calami nigrentis
Sit tuas laudes celebrare munus,
Anseris penna stolidi haud notandas,
Haud avis albas.

Dignior corvus: niger ille dicat
Te tuos nigro digitos dedisse,
Foeda nee succi timuisse obire

Probra maligni.

Candidi semper digiti manusque;
Causa nee fcedae maculae sorori
Sim, praecor cunctos superos quot extra
Tartara degunt.

Latitiam Matildam H. ita solicitat, H. H. faventibus nubibus ut obambulatum eat.

Sol poscit radiis te calidis, soror,
Daphne difficilis ne fugias Dcura;
Ah! tecum reputa quae mala virgini
Cemebant superi, crimine liberie,
Corpus per tenerum lignea fit suum!!
Tu lente residens, ut tibi mos, domi,
Phcebaeos radios tarn male dum fugis,
Ne fias, Niobes immodicae immemor,
Non laurus viridis sed gelidus lapis.

In Poetam qui de Jluviis ripas superantibus, et de quodam incendio, duo poemata haud Jeliciter scriptit.

Poeta duplex, ignem aquamque tu canis;
Non igne clarus, non aqua clarus, canis;
Ne tu puellas non volentes flagita,
Vetant Camoenae te igne tristes ac aqua.

For the ease of a foreigner, it is necessary to premise that the ensuing Latin lines are a translation of these nursery rhymes:— When I was a bachelor I lived by myself,
And all the money that I got, I put upon a shelf.
The rats and the mice they made such a strife,
I was forced to go to London to get me a wife:
The streets were so broad, and the lanes were so narrow,
I was forced to bring my wife home in a wheelbarrow:
The wheelbarrow broke, and gave my wife a fall:
The crows take the wheelbarrow, wife, and all.

Uxor nulla mihi est, en cogor vivere solus!

Sors dederit nummos? angulus ater habet. Tantos clamores dant mures nocte dieque,

Urbem adeo, uxorem (si mihi fas sit) emam. Per latos vicos iter est; iter estque per arctos;

Uxorem ducam, sors jubet — uniroti! Frangitur unirotis! nuptae mala causa cadendi:

Ad cqrvos abeant uxor et unirotis.
WITH A LATIN GRAMMAR.
Dum cupiens lingua; Romanac carpere flores,
Cara soror, versas nocte dieque libros;
    Sis prudens, animo morbi minitantur, et aiunt,
Non sanabit eos quos tibi Apollo feret..
Written under the Sign of the Blue Boy.
    Here I do stand all wind and rain:
True blue will never stain.
    Hie spiret Boreas, descendat Jupiter, aclsum:
Nulla est in lucido caeruleo macula.
On reading that the Duke of Marlborough after.the Battle of Blenheim, had marched through a barren country.
    Terra patet sterilis, cur sis per inhospita victor?-
Lauri non illic — unde corona tibi?
EPITAPH IN STEPNEY CHURCH-YARD.
See Hattons New View qf London, 1708.)
A maid near eighteen
    We have laid in this green, To rest herself here a short space;
But, after a time,
This rose in her prime,
    Shall rise up again by God's grace.
    Has sedes juxta gratas (vix attigit annos
Octodecim) miserum! pulchra puella jacet!
    Hie requiem sumat! post paulum clara, resurget
Haec rosa; sic statuit gratia magna Dei.
On seeing Buonaparte's Carriage when exhibited to the Public.
    It may be necessary to call to mind, that the coachman who drove Bonaparte to Moscow, was part of the exhibition, and that he was called John Home. How genuine this account was, must be left, without any opinion, to the judgment or information of the reader.
    Two coachmen me, when Emperor, drove, Poor plain John Home was one;
The next, all human praise above!
Th' immortal Wellington.
Two diff'rent ways they drove me forth,
(My heart, O still thy thrillings!)
The former drove me to the north,
    The latter to St. Helens.
FOR OUR HOUSE AT TWICKENHAM.
Ecce, diu adversi, tandem rediere Penates,
Huic semper sit Pax incola grata domo,
    Hinc procul amoveant damnosse jurgia linguae,
Sint procul hinc curae, sit procul oinne malum,
    Ut mihi jam fas est hilaris bona scire juventae, Mox mihi dent superi, quale senecta sciam.
    In mentioning Miss Seward, whom, as I never knew her, I do not wish to bring forward, I intended to have called up the spirit of her friend Mr. George Hardinge, who, a classical scholar himself, must surely have been far from serious in patronising her " Centenary of Odes from Horace," which she was to versify from a literal prose translation! They were, in this state, which brings to mind Chaucer's lines,
    "And many a Jack of Dover had he sold, Which had been two times hot, and two times cold," to be rendered into English verse, with the preservation of all their original spirit! What is it that some persons will not assert, and others avouch? She succeeded, as she usually did, to her *own* satisfaction; and no echo ever had the right to frame its own opinion, save that of the Irishman, which replied, "Pretty well, I thank you," when Paddy proposed, as the test of its truth, the question, " How do you do?"
    Were I to dwell long enough on Miss Seward's character, to enter into the biography of herself, or one of her coxcomical admirers — he too a servant of the Muses! I might be excited by the ruffled feather of my pen, to vent my indignation: I will calm it by going to my brother, and asking him if he can tell me any thing about that erratic star, George Hardinge.
    He gives me the following memoir: — "Of George Hardinge something may be said. That he was a man of most brilliant talents, those who were at all acquainted with him must confess; but it is scarcely possible to conceive talents less adapted to legal pursuits than his. His conversation, and in many instances, his speeches at the bar, were replete with wit and merriment. By the concurrence of fortunate circumstances, which no man even with the greatest pretension can command, and scarcely ever happen to any one, he found himself, more than once, at the very head of his profession, with profit and honours thrust upon him; but the vivacity of his temper and habits and appearance, would not permit him to avail himself of the proffered good, and others more sedulous were permitted to supplant him, contented to represent himself in the court where he was acting as Vol. i, B counsel, f a very idle fellow' and to verify the assertion by a professional life of the grossest negligence. It was to all who observed it, a matter of deep regret to see talents thus lost, for Lord Camden, a near relation of Mr. H. 's, is reported to have confessed that his talents were far superior to his own, and that if he had had steadiness, every thing was in his power; but neither what he owed to his own reputation or interest, nor all his classical reminiscences, could teach him that the Syren sloth was to be shunned; and at last he closed his reckless life in very *confined* circumstances."
    The lady to whom I owe Mrs. Piozzi's anticipated review, possessed very early, and allows me to print, the following *improviso* of Mr. Hardinge, written, it may very truly be said, on the *spur* of the occasion. It needs a few words of introduction. I give those which were given to me.
    "Messrs. Triphook and Company having directed a letter, 'To George Hardinge, Esquire, if living; if dead, to his Executors,' beginning, ' Sir or Gentlemen,' and stating, that, not having heard from Mr. Hardinge after repeated applications for settling an inclosed account, they concluded he must be dead; and if that melancholy circumstance was true, requesting that it might be settled by his executors, Mr. Hardinge immediately wrote, —
    'Oh! Messieurs Triphook, what is fear'd by you,
The melancholy circumstance is true;
For I am dead; and, more afflicting still!
My legal assets will not pay your bill.
For oh! to name it I am broken-hearted,
My mortal life, insolvent I departed;
So, gentlemen, I'm your's, without a

farthing,
For my executors and self,
  'George Hardinge,
  'P. S. Excuse the postage which these

lines will cost, The dead their franking privilege have lost'" END OF THE FIRST VOLUME.

  London:

Printed by A. & R. Spottiswoode,
New-Street-Square.

CPSIA information can be obtained at www.ICGtesting.com
Printed in the USA
BVOW07s1059070314

346996BV00009B/298/P

9 781150 152252